PUBLISHED BY BOOM BOOKS

www.boombooks.biz

ABOUT THIS SERIES

....But after that, I realised that I knew very little about these parents of mine. They had been born about the start of the Twentieth Century, and they died in 1970 and 1980. For their last 20 years, I was old enough to speak with a bit of sense.

I could have talked to them a lot about their lives. I could have found out about the times they lived in. But I did not. I know almost nothing about them really. Their courtship? Working in the pits? The Lock-out in the Depression? Losing their second child? Being dusted as a miner? The shootings at Rothbury? My uncles killed in the War? Love on the dole? There were hundreds, thousands of questions that I would now like to ask them. But, alas, I can't. It's too late.

Thus, prompted by my guilt, I resolved to write these books. They describe happenings that affected people, real people. The whole series is, to coin a modern phrase, designed to push your buttons, to make you remember and wonder at things forgotten.

The books might just let nostalgia see the light of day, so that oldies and youngies will talk about the past and re-discover a heritage otherwise forgotten. Hopefully, they will spark discussions between generations, and foster the asking and answering of questions that should not remain unanswered.

BORN IN 1941?
WHAT ELSE HAPPENED?

RON WILLIAMS

AUSTRALIAN SOCIAL HISTORY

BOOK 3 IN A SERIES OF 33

FROM 1939 to 1971

War Babies Years (1939 to 1945):	**7 Titles**
Baby Boom Years (1946 to 1960):	**15 Titles**
Post Boom Years (1961 to 1971):	**11 Titles**

BOOM, BOOM BABY, BOOM

BORN IN 1941? WHAT ELSE HAPPENED?

Published by Boom Books. Wickham, NSW, Australia
Web: boombooks.biz
Email: email@boombooks.biz

Creator: Williams, Ron, 1934- author

Title: Born in 1941? What else happened? Edition: Premier edition

ISBN: 9780648771647

Cover images: National Archives of Australia. M4294, 3/1, 8852030, Holt after he introduced Child Endowment; B5919, 18/1 5951010, World War 2 Camp Postal Facilities; M2127, 1, 8847204, with Dame Annabelle Ranking at Flying Boat Base; K1131, W597A, 31325219, Forrest Post Office Inspection Party.

TABLE OF CONTENTS

IMPORTANT PEOPLE AND RECORDS

King of England	King George VI
Prime Minister of Australia:	
Until August	Bob Menzies
Until October	Arthur Fadden
After October 7th	John Curtin
Leader of the Opposition:	
Until October 7	**John Curtin**
After October 7	**Arthur Fadden**
Governor General	**Lord Gowrie**
Pope	**Pius XII**
PM of England	**Winston Churchill**
President of America	**Franklin Roosevelt**

WINNER OF THE ASHES

1936	Australia 3 - 2
1938	Drawn 1 - 1
1946	Australia 3 - 0

MELBOURNE CUP WINNERS

1940	Old Rowley
1941	Skipton
1942	Colonus

ACADEMY AWARDS

Best Actor	James Stewart
Best Actress	Ginger Rogers
Best Movie	Philadelphia Story

INTRODUCTION TO THE SERIES

I was five years old when the War started. But even at that early age, I was aware of the dread, and yet excitement, that such an epoch-making event brought to my small coal-mining town. At the start, it was not certain that it would affect us at all, but quickly it became obvious that everybody in the nation would be seriously involved in it. The most immediate response I remember was that all the Mums (who still remembered **WW1)** were worried that their sons and husbands would be taken away and killed. After that, I can remember radio speeches given by Chamberlain, Churchill, Lyons, Menzies, and Curtin telling of hard times ahead, but promising certain victory over our wicked foes.

For a young boy, as the War years went on, reality and fantasy went hand in hand. As I heard of our victories, I day-dreamed of being at the head of our Military forces, throwing grenades and leading bayonet charges. I sank dozens of battleships from my submarine that was always under attack. And I lost count of the squadrons of Messerschmitts that I sent spiralling from the sky. Needless to say, I was awarded a lot of medals and, as I got a bit older, earned the plaudits of quite a few pretty girls.

But, mixed in with all this romance were some more analytical thoughts. Every day, once the battles got going, I would go to the newspapers' maps of where the battlelines currently were. One for the Western front, one in North Africa, and a third in Russia. Later, another in the Pacific. Then I would examine them minutely to see just how far we had moved, backwards or forwards. I read all the reports, true and false, and gloated when it was said we were winning, and shrunk away from our losses.

At the personal level, I remember the excitement of getting up at 4am on a few days when nearby Newcastle was under submarine attack. We went to our underground air-raid shelter that we shared with a neighbour, and listened, and occasionally looked out, for some who-knows-what enemies to appear. It really was a bit scary. I can remember too the brown-outs, and the black-outs, the searchlights, the tank-traps, the clackers that were given to wardens to warn of gas attacks, and the gasmasks that 20 town-wardens (only) carried, presumably to save a town of 2,000 people when needed. Then there was the rationing, the shortages of everything, and even the very short shirt tails that a perceptive Government decreed were necessary to win the War.

At the start of researching this book, everything began to come back to me. Things such as those above, and locations like Dunkirk, Tobruk, El Alamein, Stalingrad, and Normandy. Really, at this stage these names kept popping up, but I was at loss as to how significant they were. Also, names of people. Hitler and Mussolini I knew were baddies. But **how** bad? Chamberlain was always criticised for his appeasement, but what were his alternatives? Who **were** Ribbentrop and Molotov, and Tojo and Blamey, and what was Vichy France?

And finally, when war did come, and grind on, year after year, what effect did it have back here in Australia? How did we as a society cope with a world that just had to continue on, given that the sons and dads of the nation were actually being killed daily overseas? When the postman did his normal delivery and brought a letter saying your loved one is dead? What did we do when old jobs suddenly disappeared, and new ones were created a hundred miles away? When goods, long readily available, were no longer for sale? When everything changed?

It was all a hotch-potch to me when I started this series. At the end of it, I can say it is a lot clearer. I have sorted out the countable things like battles, locations, people, and rules and regulations. I can appreciate, too, the effects on society, though these can only be ascertained from what I **have** researched, and make no allowance for all that I have missed.

In presenting each book, I have started many chapters with a visit to Europe, and a look at the military events in the world, with increasing emphasis on the Pacific. Then I come back to Oz to see how we are faring in a military sense. After that, I blunder about reporting and speculating on which aspects of life here were affected by these, and other ongoing matters.

So, despite all the talk about the War above, and despite the fact that it was the controlling influence on all of our lives, the thrust of these books is about **the social changes and reactions that took place in this period, here in Oz.**

THE SOURCES OF MY MATERIAL

I was born in 1934, so that I can remember well a great deal of what went on around me from 1939 onwards. But of course, the bulk of this book's material came from research. That meant that I spent many hours in front of a computer reading electronic versions of newspapers, magazines, Hansard, Ministers' Press releases and the like. My task was to sift out, day-by-day, those stories and events that would be of interest to the most readers. Then I supplemented these with materials from books, broadcasts, memoirs, biographies, government reports and statistics. And I talked to old-timers, one-on-one, and in organised groups, and to Baby Boomers about their recollections. People with stories to tell came out of the woodwork, and talked no end about the tragic, and funny, and commonplace events that have shaped their very different lives.

The presentation of each book. For each year covered, the end result is a collection of short Chapters on many of the topics that concerned ordinary people in that year. **I think I have covered most of the major issues that people then were interested in**. On the other hand, **in some cases I have dwelt a little on minor frivolous matters**, perhaps to the detriment of more sober considerations. Still, in the long run, this makes the book more readable, and hopefully it will convey adequately the spirit of the times.

Each of the books is mainly Sydney based, but I have been deliberately national in outlook, so that readers elsewhere will feel comfortable that I am talking about matters that affected them personally. After all, housing shortages and strikes and juvenile delinquency involved all Australians, and other issues, such as problems overseas, had no State component in them. Overall, **I expect I can make you wonder, remember, rage and giggle equally, no matter where you hail from**.

EUROPE'S LEGACY FROM EARLIER YEARS

Britain and Europe. Britain had survived a brutal year in 1940. At the beginning of that year, her own and the French armies were fairly happily ensconced in the Maginot Line of defences, on the German border, keeping out of the winter weather, and playing peek-a-boo with similar German forces holed up about twenty miles away in their Siegfried Line. For about five months, on either side of Christmas, war activity on this front, along the entire French border, had stopped and both sides were enjoying what was being called **the Phoney War**.

But as the 1940-snow thawed, the Germans came out of their hibernation by invading and conquering Norway, Luxemburg, Denmark, Holland, and Belgium. She had done most of all this by early May. A few weeks later, the British troops, who had come out of their Line to protect the above nations, were cornered on the coast of France at **Dunkirk**. They were evacuated from there, under enemy fire, by a flotilla of large and small craft, and over a period of about a week, 438,000 British and French troops were thus evacuated back to England. Every episode in the War so far that year had ended in fiasco, and given the huge loss of face at Dunkirk, the British Prime Minister, Neville Chamberlain resigned. His place was taken by Winston Churchill.

Then Russia got into the swing of things, and "persuaded' the Baltic states Estonia, Latvia and Lithuania to join her in a Soviet State, and then she fought and won a bloody war with Finland. A bit more colour, and getting quite impressive.

Germany was at the cetrre of Europe. She had common borders with about a dozen other smaller and weaker nation, and by now they had nearly all come under the military control of their bully neighbour. But France was a bit different.

WHAT HAPPENED TO FRANCE?

Back to early June, 1940, the British had been evacuated from Dunkirk, and the French Army was in retreat and confusion. Hitler then simply moved his troops southwards on a wide front, defeating the French as he went, and by June 12 they had reached the outskirts of Paris. Over the next ten days, the French officially capitulated and delivered the south of France, as well as Paris, peacefully into German hands. Thereafter the Government of the southern half of France was controlled from the **small city of Vichy**, and was more or less collaborative with the Germans. In any case, for the British, **France was suddenly and completely out of the War**. It was not at all certain whether her troops might change sides, and turn on the British at a later stage.

The Brits were aghast at this turn of events. Their major ally, who had promised to fight to the death, and who for years had acted as the potential co-policeman of Europe, had capitulated with a lot less struggle than several of the smaller nations had waged. Some Brits felt betrayed. Others said that the French had no choice. The French themselves were equally confused.

The new French **Government** had decided on the Armistice. **The people** did not know whether to laugh or cry. None of them wanted war, and the Armistice removed any worry about this, and about their nation being pillaged. On the other hand, they had been expecting to fight to the finish, and perhaps winning, and conquering the Nazis. Now they had to suffer, or perhaps not suffer, German domination in a velvet glove. Perhaps, most of them thought, it might work out. In any case, what could any one person do?

By the time that July 1940 came, you might have thought that the Brits would have had enough. But you would have been wrong, very wrong. And anyway, Hitler had his own ideas of what was a fair thing.

WHAT HITLER DID NEXT

The Fuhrer decided he should invade Britain. It was a logical thing to do. After all, he had just flogged her forces in open battle and sent them scurrying home. He had more planes than Britain, and all he had to do was cross a narrow Channel. So he launched never-ending air attacks on Britain to soften her up. For two months, he sent huge numbers of aircraft to attack her harbours, ports, military bases, and later London and the cities. This period was called the Battle of Britain, and the London Blitz, and at the end, Hitler was trying to break the spirit of the British with constant air raids.

From mid July until mid September, this Battle raged. The Royal Air Force (RAF) every day fought tirelessly against the would-be invader, and every day lost only half the planes that the Germans lost. By mid-September, Hitler had had enough, and he called off the invasion. He kept up the bombing until May 1941, but at a much reduced rate, and he never looked like breaking the spirit of the Brits. As far as invasion of their shores was concerned, Britain could rest easily.

MUSSOLINI WANTED HIS SHARE.

Benito had been slow to join Germany. He had ultimately declared war against the Allies only in June 1940, when it was clear that France was about to stop fighting. Then in

November, he annoyed his new comrade-in-arms, Hitler, by invading Greece.

Over the next two months, up till Christmas 1940, he suffered three major blows. **First**, the Greeks, with some British help, forced his Armies out of Greece and back into Albania. **Second**, half of his very good fleet was destroyed by the British in the Battle of Taranto. **Third**, at about that time, our own AIF Forces got into action at last and saved Egypt from Italian occupation, and won handsome victories over the Italians in Libya. These were tough blows to Mussolini, and spoiled his Christmas. We will come back to these later in this book.

THE BRIT NAVY AND AIR FORCE?

While all this was going on, Germany had caused distressing damage at sea. In good news for the Brits, half the German fleet had been destroyed in Norway, and her above-surface fleet gave very little trouble after that. But her **submarines** were very effective and destroyed hundreds of Royal Navy and merchant vessels. Also, her magnetic mines took a big toll. The Brits countered by using the convoy system, and by employing mine-sweepers, and gradually added efficient radar to their ships. But the subs were still a great menace at the start of 1941.

The Air Force had fought and won the Battle of Britain. Her losses in manpower and planes had been substantial, but replacement planes were coming from Britain's own factories, and from America. Her man-power was being topped-up by new recruits from Australia and the British Dominions, under an Empire-based scheme. For the last six months, the RAF had been raiding strategic targets in Germany, and had recently moved on to Italy.

THE BRITS AT HOME

By some miraculous process, the Brits were still alive. A lot of the men-folk had been killed and maimed in the Services and the merchant Navy. **A total of 43,000 civilians were killed in the bombings, and one million houses were destroyed**. People, especially in London, had spent innumerable hours in air raid shelters.

Country centres, such as Coventry, had been virtually destroyed. London children had been taken away to the country, away from their parents. Then they had come back again. And after that, the whole family had gone to the country. Add to that, rationing, and shortages, gasmasks, blackouts, propaganda and censorship, officialdom, and the curtailment of cherished liberties. Yet the Brits survived. Their spirit was intact, their resolve undaunted. It was this resolve, the resolve that France did not have, that beat the Germans. It was indeed a miracle.

A NOTE ON OUR NEWSPAPERS

The Australian Government and authorities were running campaigns of all sorts to encourage people to spend less, and to consume less. They were also told to salvage iron, aluminium, and old clothing, and make their cars last a few more years. One particular form of austerity related to daily newspapers. At the start of the War, the *Sydney Morning Herald* was typically 25 pages. Now it was down to 15. The composition of the news changed, too. Before the War, there was great deal of reporting of minor, often silly events from the suburbs and towns. Now, most of this was gone, and was replaced with matters military and overseas War news. This was much more grave and portentous, and a lot of it was blatant propaganda from disguised Government sources. Still, I am happy to say, our newspapers kept a level head throughout the War, and maintained their freedom in a balanced and sensible way.

MY RULES IN WRITING

I give you a few Rules that I follow as I write. They will help you understand where I am coming from.

Rule One. Throughout this book, I rely a lot on reproducing Letters from the newspapers. Whenever I do this, I put the text in a different font, and indent it a little, and make the font somewhat smaller. I do not edit the text at all. **That is, I do not correct spelling or if the text gets at all garbled, I do not correct it. It's just as it was seen in the Papers.**

Second Rule. The material for this book, when it comes from newspapers, is reported as it was seen at the time. If the benefit of hindsight over the years changes things, then I might record that in my Comments. **The info reported thus reflects matters as they were seen in 1941.**

Third Rule. Let me also apologise in advance to anyone I might offend. In a work such as this, **it is certain some people will think I got some things wrong. I am sure that I did**, but please remember, all of **this is only my opinion**. And really, **my** opinion does not matter one little bit in the scheme of things. **I hope you will say "silly old bugger", and shrug your shoulders, and read on.**

So now we are ready to plunge into 1941. Let's go, and I trust you will have a pleasant trip.

JANUARY: THE WAR IN OZ

Australia had changed greatly during 1940. As events in Europe unfolded, and as our soldiers left our shores, and as our Airmen arrived in Britain, people got more serious about the War. Some people got really fanatical about it, and wanted other people to give up horse racing, football, dances, jazz, greyhound racing, new clothing, and even the Melbourne Cup. Some people were branding others as cowards if they were not seen in military uniform. But generally, patriotism was high and rising, but not to extreme levels.

The newspapers were full of news connected with the War. Men in uniforms were everywhere, and the young girls thought this marvellous. New jobs were being created in factories for these young maidens, and many of them became drivers, mechanics, firemen, ambulance officers, and clerks. Their world was suddenly very different, and **this** was the start of Womens' Lib.

On the economic front, more and more materials were going to the War effort. Taxation had been hugely increased just before Christmas to pay for all this, and War Loans were constantly asking citizens to lend money to the Government to help it out. Petrol rationing was moderately severe, and there was a growing scarcity of spare parts, and indeed mechanics, to keep old vehicles on the road. Our shortage of ready spending money meant that our reserves of overseas currencies were running out, so that our imports were being restricted. New cars would soon be off the menu.

Amidst this austerity, the population was happy enough, though a lot of people were permanently worried. Parents and wives of families whose menfolk had been sent overseas were the worst hit. But anyone who had someone in the Services knew that before long, their men would get on a boat and be gone. They were plagued by the thought that they might never return. Sadly, they were all too often correct.

Still everyone had some degree of worry. It just gnawed away, it was there in the background every day, and especially every night. Would Britain succumb? If it did, then surely Australia would have to surrender. Would the War last for long? No one at this stage imagined that it would go on for another four and a half years. Would the War machine in Oz gobble up those men who were **now** exempt from Service? Perhaps even old Dad might get the call-up. Everyone had their own fear, and it just quietly nagged away all the time.

We really should also have been worried about events to our North, emanating from Japan. This country had for about three years clearly been in a bellicose mood, and had captured a third of China. It was trying to bully the nations of Indo- China, and was making growling noises at the USA and Britain. Its every move in 1940 should have worried us, but we found it unbelievable that it could and would take up arms against us, and the USA, and south east Asia, and the Pacific.

So as the year 1941 commenced, we were totally unworried by this thought, and had our Christmas and New Year, and the next month of indolence and happiness, fully believing that all the threats to our shores came from 12,000 miles away. And that was so far away, that there was really no threat at all.

Sadly, reality was just about to dawn on us, and by the end of 1941, our concerns were more with our own shores than with those of Britain.

ANZACS IN NORTH AFRICA

Libya was an **Italian** colony in the north of Africa, next door to Egypt and the Suez Canal.. Benito Mussolini, the Duce, was **anxious to prove his military capabilities**, and he wanted control of the Canal. So, in November 1940, he invaded Egypt and was only 500 miles from its capital in Cairo. But, his progress was slow and by mid-December the main body of his troops had advanced less than 200 miles.

Then, the British Forces staged a counter-attack. Firstly, they stopped the Italian advance in battles at Sidi Barrani. Then as the Italians retreated to their fortified positions in Libya, **the Australian Imperial Forces** (AIF) had stunning victories at Bardia, then at the port of Tobruk, and moving westward, at Derna, and Benghazi. On February 8th, they were halfway across Libya, and crying out for permission to continue to the west, and take all of Libya and its capital Tripoli. It turned out, as we shall see, that permission was never given.

BACK IN BRITAIN

These victories were just what the doctor ordered for Britain. **Firstly**, it was wonderful to have battles move away from their own shores to somewhere else. It meant for certain that Britain would not be invaded, at least in the short term, and after months of deep and widespread fear, this was a great relief.

Secondly, the roles that Australia, New Zealand, and India played in the great wins were like a tonic. Britain had lost France as an ally, but she had gained the Empire as a better substitute. Newsreels showing the triumphs in movie theatres were loudly cheered as the Empire forces paraded.

Thirdly, this was the **first** land victory that Britain had been a party to in this War. She had in fact suffered half a dozen land defeats in just over a year, and to have such a convincing win now was pennies from heaven.

JAPAN AND ASIA: NEWS AND VIEWS

Japan invaded China in 1937, and had taken over most of that nation's ports. Currently she also had control of a large area of desolate land in the northwest, which she had conquered and then named Manchukuo. The battles for the remainder of China were on a large scale, and were ongoing, with more and more land gradually falling to the Flag of the Rising Sun.

Over the last six months, Japan had been active elsewhere. On the diplomatic front, **she had signed a Pact with Germany and Italy, promising mutual support** under certain conditions. It had no practical significance at the moment, but it put Japan **firmly in the camp of the Axis powers,** and very definitely at odds with Britain and America. Also recently, she had been rattling her sword in Indo-China (Vietnam, Cambodia, and Laos), where the withdrawal of France from the War left that area uncertain of ongoing French protection. There was a similar situation on the scattered islands of Indonesia, where the Dutch colonists were of dubious value as a military force. Japan was not quite licking her lips, but she was at least wetting them.

On January 9, the *Sydney Morning Herald* took stock of the Japanese situation in an Editorial. It pointed out that the

moderate Government of Japan was perhaps losing control of the Army, and that Nazi agents were now influential in that Army, and were working to draw Japan into the War against Britain. It went on to say that the doctrine of **a Co-prosperity Sphere** was being promised throughout Asia under a new Japanese hegemony, but this really meant **conquest by the Japanese Imperial forces, and the usurpation of all property and rights**.

This represented a hardening of attitude by the *SMH.* Other Australian newspapers followed suit. At the same time, they started to publish Letters that questioned and criticised Japan's motives for its clearly intemperate actions. But **there was no appreciation of the fact that we had an errant military colossus to our north**, and that we should be immediately wary of it.

> **Letters, (Mrs) Bertha Wilkie, Dee Why.** I was amazed to read the statement by the Minister for External Affairs, claiming "cordial relations" between Australia and Japan! Is Sir Frederick Stewart aware of the fact that, as his predecessor in office said, Japan has signed a military alliance with our enemies? Does this Minister imagine for one minute that he is voicing the sentiments of the majority of Australians, and, particularly, those of the wives and mothers of our AIF men abroad? The people are entitled to an answer to these questions.
>
> So far, Mr Spender seems to be "the right man in the right job," yet he goes too far when he states that "Australia has no quarrel with Japan." Certainly, we wish to live on friendly terms with Japan, but

only if she conducts herself in such a way that friendly relations between us may continue.

When Japan scraps the military alliance with Hitler and cuts herself absolutely adrift from the Axis, thereby proving that her southward expansion would be peaceful and economic, then, perhaps, will just grounds be discovered for "cordial relations" between Australia and Japan.

I am certain my husband in Palestine and my son in the 8th Division, do not think "cordial relations" exist between us and Japan. Still, there may be more in both these statements than meet the eye. Let us hope so, anyway.

Letters, H Jones. Even Japan, intent upon making herself the colossus of the Pacific, cannot have it both ways. When she browbeat Korea and later swarmed into Manchuria and China, she assured the world that she was compelled to find more space for the teeming millions who were suffocating in her own confined area. Today, we are told that she is developing a social scheme for the express purpose of increasing her population by many millions.

Maybe Western economics are changing the whole course of life in the Far East. While in Honolulu, I learnt that Japanese immigrants usually started with families of ten children, but in the second generation the figure dropped to four or five. With the expansion of manufacturing industries, the birth rate has gradually fallen in Japan. To arrest this drop would be a national duty in any country, but it is the military party which is in power in Tokyo, and its plans to force the population up by some twenty millions indicate that its ideas are not centripetal, but centrifugal. Plainly they seek additional nationals to police the new possessions, direct and indirect, which they covet, so they may be controlled by their own conquering race.

OZ MILITARY: NEWS AND VIEWS

Strikes in war-time. There was a considerable number of people who thought that **strikes in wartime** were reprehensible, or criminal or even treason. Below are Letters from typical advocates of this view.

Letters, A Walker. What foolish people we are in Australia. We let the talker have full sway, and we are slow to think for ourselves. As workers and members of Unions, we allow ourselves to be led by others without a protest, even though we are certain in our own minds that we are being misled. Here we are demanding extra conditions, and tolerating stoppages, while our sons and brothers have gone to the front to face the enemy. Raiders are in our seas, grave dangers are confronting us, the homeland is at grips with a powerful foe, but the workers of Australia are living in a fool's paradise. We turn a deaf ear to grave warnings that, should the enemy win, then our liberty is gone.

I appeal to the workers of Australia to stand by the Government in this critical time in our history. Our duty is to do our job cheerfully and faithfully.

Letters, Disgusted, Sydney. Australians, what is wrong with us? Like hundreds of thousands of others in our State, I have just been listening to the broadcast about the glorious achievements of our boys at the fall of Bardia. Did any loyal citizen listen to that and not get a thrill? Then we heard the contents of the cable advising that the casualties were light, probably not more than 500, presumably killed and wounded. Then, almost with the next breath, we heard a long list of strikes, in our State, all affecting our war efforts.

Visualise for a minute those boys, lying dead in Northern Africa, having given all, so that we might continue to enjoy freedom. **Yet the strikers refuse to work**, thus holding up supplies for our soldiers to use, in that fight for our freedom, which includes those strikers. Lord, give us men!

If lives are lost through lack of munitions and equipment, etc, production of which must assuredly be seriously curtailed by these systematic strikes, then these lives must be laid at the doors of the strikers. Have they ever thought of this, or are they so blind or unconcerned that they can send our lads away and then deprive them of the means whereby they are to fight?

Are we all so blind that we cannot see that if England falls, then Australia is doomed, and all the advantages and privileges we enjoy will disappear very quickly and not all the strikes in the world will bring them back again?

Comment. You can bet that if lives were lost "through lack of munitions and equipment", the newspapers and politicians would have been quick to let us know. Their complete silence in this respect tells us that such concerns were fanciful.

The workers saw things differently. This Letter was published by the *Newcastle Herald*, which was much better disposed to the workers than was the *SMH*.

Letters, Keith Todd, Heddon Greta. The many writers criticising strikers in the Sydney papers should try for a few facts. In my pit, where we are genuinely producing more coal for no extra pay, we were last week told to work a seam that had been **standing idle for twenty years**. Back then, we had worked it for a few weeks, and found it to be less than five feet high, full of deadly gas, and the roof had floater after floater that meant we were at constant risk of death. The seam was closed by agreement with the management.

Now we are being told to work it. **The argument is that it is for the war effort.** Of course, there is plenty of other coal still available, and the only reason for this order is so that the bosses can make money out of a worthless asset. We refused to work the seam, and said we will continue to work the rest of the pit as normal. We were stood down. The next day, Sydney papers reported us on strike, and the Editorial and letter writers abused us again.

It's the old story. Capital versus Labour. If management can exploit any situation for profit, it will. It doesn't matter to them if it is a War, just anything will do.

Comment. This Letter, and similar ones from other industries, made arguments that were worth listening to. However "the matrons from Mosman" and elsewhere persisted in writing Letters against strikers, and the newspapers continued to publish them with glee.

Then there was another strike matter that raised its head. It was over **the tax on hours of overtime worked**. The Taxation system was different from that of today, and the

Federal tax was calculated on a day's pay, so that if you worked nine hours a day you were taxed at a certain rate, but if you worked 14 hours, you were taxed **for the full 14 hours** at a substantially higher rate. Various bodies, such as the Sheet Metal workers objected to this, and said that it was not fair that the first nine hours should be taxed at the higher rate. That meant, for those hours, they were losing money by working overtime.

As the weeks progressed more Unionists came to this opinion, and it started to become a big industrial problem. Again, the Letter writers chimed in. I include this rather special one.

Letters, Mary Condon. Workers are once again endangering our men overseas by refusing to work overtime. Apart from the callous selfishness in leaving them without the means of staying alive, I draw attention to their own folly in not working. All that is asked is for them to work **an extra 20 hours per wee**k. Do they not know that our men overseas are working 168 hours per week every week. These so-called workers should work the extra 20 hours per week without asking any money at all, and then they would be doing their bit. Until then, they should be ashamed of themselves, and go out and enlist themselves.

A more moderate tone was possible, as shown below.

Letters, Stoker. Greedy employers are equally prone to use the exigency of war rampantly to exploit labour and smash its machinery of representation as over-zealous trade unionists might be to attain industrial rights before national security.

I have worked shoulder to shoulder with men in the key industries. Recently, I've seen them work at a terrific pace – to the point of exhaustion! Some working seven days a week with short breaks at change of shift; others on 12-hour shifts, who go home to a meal and go to bed, to get up and go to work again. An endless, ungrudging task shared alike by the manager and the worker. And because of this sharing the effort I've seen production figures rise to staggering heights. The men who accomplish these feats are not agitators, neither are they senseless beasts of burden. They are honest men with legitimate rights, which include the democratic privilege of rejecting impositions or even imputations of injustice.

All that can be gleaned from the present industrial unrest is that unsatisfactory conditions exist and that the machinery of consultation is faulty. Until this is rectified, strike and the threat of strike is the only weapon the working man can wield.

Letters, J Morrison. I think there are few fair-minded people who do not sympathise with the man who, by working overtime at the requests of his employer and for his country, places a much higher rate of taxation upon the wages he has earned in his regular hours, together with a similar charge upon the portion received for overtime.

All we are asking for is a proper chance to discuss it. As far as we can see, no Government Minister, including the Prime Minister, is prepared to give us an audience, because if he does, he will see our point of view and he will bear the odium of being seen to give way to the workers. So none of them will come near a conference table, and simply brand us as traitors.

Letters, Helen Simmons. And what is "a worker". Is he not an ordinary person like you or me? Do we all not work to live and, living, look to the light of freedom and to a better world? But this freedom we search for must be earned. We in Australia have plenty of it, by the grace of God, and of England. If we desire more, then let us earn it by works, not ranting.

Let us have done with all this mummery. Either one is for Britain and freedom, or one is for Hitler and bondage. If our Government is not strong and brave enough to smite the hand which pulls its nose, then we might as well all go haywire and pull it out of office, working on the principle that what followed could hardly be worse. Let us define clearly what is a worker, let us cooperate in steadiness of purpose, learn to pay our taxes, and shut up about it.

THE JAVA APE MAN

There was still controversy over the origin of the universe and life. We still had Darwinism under various names, and equally there was quite a revival of various forms of Creationism. Back in 1941, the topic was very hot indeed, and anyone who wanted an argument could get one at the drop of a hat.

I have included three Letters, two of them from the one writer. I have excluded their technical arguments because they get so abstruse that today's outsider could not hope to follow them. I have, however, included the terms of endearment that they threw around liberally, so that you can get an idea of how hot the topic was.

Letters, Robert Watsford. Professor Eugene Dubois discovered in 1891 three teeth, a tiny fragment of a lower jaw, and two fragments of the top of the skull. From these relics a cast of the "Java Ape Man" was reconstructed with the aid of plaster of Paris and even larger amounts of imagination!

Nearly a million persons in New York annually view this bundle of imagination and look upon it as their ancestor, notwithstanding the fact that the discoverer, Professor Dubois, in 1935, declared "that after all, he was satisfied the relics were not of a man but of a Gibbon (monkey)." The fatuous faith and infantile credulity of the evolutionary public is astounding.

Letters, David Stead. In a clumsy attempt to bring ridicule upon the results of long and patient investigation by scientific anthropologists and the most distinguished anatomists, your correspondent, Robert Watsford, speaks smartly of "the fatuous faith and infantile credulity of the evolutionary public" (sic!).

Well, the investigators who "restored" the Java Ape Man were neither the victims of fatuous faith nor of infantile credulity, but instead, possessed a profound knowledge of scientific method and comparative anatomy.

Whether the remains were those of a large Gibbon makes not a whit of difference to the general study and conclusions regarding the ascent of man from the ape. Sir Arthur Keith considered that Java Ape Man was "a being human in stature, human in gait, human in all parts save its brain." There can be but little doubt that it was of humanoid stock, or very near to such.

Whatever your correspondent means by the "evolutionary public" I cannot pretend to guess, but the facts of evolution are too well established – by the work of many thousands of scientists – for there to be any room for cavil.

Letters, Robert Watsford. All the bones purporting to belong to the Java Ape Man, the Neanderthal, Heidelberg, and the Piltdown "fake" would not make a complete skeleton or a skull. Mr Stead does not hesitate to endorse the widest guesses of the evolutionists. He sits upon the pyramid of doubt and proclaims without a blush that ...... His remarks are typical of Darwin, who uses phrases of doubt about 800 times in his two principal works and also of H G Wells, who employs 96 expressions of uncertainty to show man's descent from an ape-like ancestry in his "Outline of History."

Dr Etheridge, famous fossilogist, one of the highest world authorities, said, "the talk of evolutionists is sheer nonsense, not founded on observation and wholly unsupported by facts." Huxley, Fleischmann, Kelvin, and others without limit, are also of similar mind.

Comment. Over the years since 1941, evolution has become more accepted than it was then.

FEBRUARY: EUROPE IN SPRING

The Military Forces of Italy occupied centre stage in February. Their armies were getting a belting in Libya and East Africa against the British Empire, and in Albania against the Greeks. Their navy was losing out against the Brits on the Mediterranean. Italian cities were being bombed, off and on, by the RAF.

Hitler did not like this at all. He had conquered most of mainland Europe without any serious challenge. Then his win-hungry ally Mussolini had gone off and attacked Greece and was now copping a pasting from that country. At the same time, his military adventures on the continent of Africa had all gone bad. **Italy had become a severe embarrassment to Hitler.** Perhaps, through Mussolini's various fiascos, the idea might get around that Hitler too might be readily beaten. Said Hitler "The defeat of Italian troops in Albania and Greece has struck a blow at the belief of our invincibility, that was previously held by friend and foe alike"

Hitler, though, had his own agenda. His focus had moved from Britain in the west, to his good and trusted ally, Russia, in the east. **Here he had changed his programme slightly.** About a year ago he had made a number of alliances with Stalin that said they would not attack each other, and might sometimes help each other in battle. This seemed like good insurance to Hitler, who was, at that time, intent on scuttling France and Britain in the west. But this little task was no longer high on his priority list, so he could jettison his treaties with Russia, and turn them into a spectacular act of treachery.

So, as I said above, he changed his programme slightly. In fact, it was a **bit** more than "slightly". He decided instead that he would launch a secret full-scale attack on Russia. He had his various military chiefs prepare flat out, and by the end of February, all was well in hand for grand military action when the winter was over. The invasion was to be called **Operation Barbarossa, and was scheduled to start on May 15th.**

Now, however, Mussolini's situation interfered with the planning. As February turned to March, Hitler was becoming more and more worried by Italian defeats. The only way he could turn the battles was to send his own German troops in to take over. But that involved two major questions of policy.

The first question involved Greece. If he wanted to put his troops into Greece, he would have to move them across Hungary, and the Balkan states of Yugoslavia, Bulgaria, and Romania. These were still independent States, and though very frightened of Hitler's forces, would probably resist the passage of his troops. So the first policy question considered was how to get this assent.

The second question was how to stop the Brits from driving west in Libya, and capturing all of that country. There was an easy solution to this, and again, it would involve the use of German troops. So, General Erwin Rommel, the ***Desert Fox***, was appointed to lead the Germans in an assault on Empire Forces there, and on February 12th he flew to the Libyan capital of Tripoli, on the western coastal edge of Libya.

BRITAIN'S MAJOR DECISION ON FEB 12th.

While all of this was exercising Hitler's brain, Winston Churchill came to a momentous decision. As we saw last month, the Empire Forces had ripped across Libya, had recently captured Benghazi, and were anxious to go on to complete the job at Tripoli. Churchill decided to **halt the advance on North Africa, and send forces instead to Greece**.

He reasoned that although the Greeks had won great victories against the Italians, they were almost exhausted, and he feared that Germany would soon join the fray. "It would be wrong to abandon the Greeks, who were putting up a magnificent fight, and were prepared to fight the Germans." So, at the same time that Hitler was preparing to throw his military might against the Empire Forces in Libya, Churchill started to withdraw his troops from that scene, and send them to Greece. **This proved to be one of the great strategic miscalculations of the War. Especiallyfor Australian troops thereabouts.**

MENZIES OVERSEAS

Robert Menzies, Oz Prime Minister, had left Australia in early February for an indefinite time to go to Europe. He had spent several weeks in Egypt and Libya, sharing the glory of our victories there, and then proceeded to England, where he mixed with Churchill, and the other high and mighty. He was much in demand as a dinner-speaker, and his rousing messages about the glory of our troops, were well received back home.

But now, he would be tested. Churchill and his War Lords, **were looking to Australians to work miracles**. In particular, they were scheduled to go to Greece for what was, at best, a difficult task, to take on the German Army and Air Force. The equipment that our Forces (with the New Zealanders) had was clearly insufficient for the task. Would Menzies, and the Oz General Thomas Blamey, be able somehow to use their **political** skills to avert the defeats that were clearly a possibility?

But, while Menzies played in Britain, his Deputy, Arthur Fadden, stirred the pot on a few issues that Menzies had kept clear of.

Firstly, he gave the nation a more relistic impression of the growing danger of Japan. On February 13th, he issued a statement that suddenly widened the scope of the defences we needed. He started, as usual, with reference to the threat from Germany. Then in cautious language, **he ventured into new territory**.

"We find ourselves in serious danger of hostile enemy action near, if not on, **our own shoreline**. It is not an unavoidable danger, far from it, but it is certainly real and we must pay serious and urgent regard to it....within a relatively short time, we can make this country so strong that no single power will care to attack it."

In retrospect, it is easy to quibble over aspects of this speech. For example, he was obliquely warning us against the Japanese, **together with Germany**, attacking our shores. It had not occurred to authorities that Japan **herself**, **without any reference to Axis allies**, might become a predator. Also, he seemed to think that we could make ourselves immune from attack in "a relatively short time."

The fact that he was wrong on both these counts, and others, does not detract from his main message. That was that Japan was to be seen as a real threat, and that Australia must prepare more earnestly for **attack of its own shores. And that this attack might be expected soon.**

Secondly, Fadden also got **the Labor leader, John Curtin, to join the War Council**. This was something Curtin would not do under Menzies. It meant that, for the first time, **the two major political parties were pooling their war efforts**, and so one impediment to efficiency was removed. At last, the Letter writers sighed, there is a bit of sense in our planning.

GROWING DISLIKE OF MENZIES

The Government in Oz was under the control of the United Party, led by Robert Menzies. He was pretty uneasy in the job because he scarcely had the numbers in Parliament. In fact, he could just muster enough votes only because he had the support of the Country Party and two Independents. Also, within his own Party there was constant dissension, so all the time he was looking over his shoulder. Trouble for Bob was on the horizen.

The Opposition was the Labor Party, led by John Curtin. The big policy difference with Menzies was over conscription of men, and their use overseas. **Curtin said not likely. Menzies sent off shiploads as soon as they were half ready.** This was a matter that would become of critical importance in the future.

BRITAIN HITS THE JACKPOT

On February 9th, the US Congress passed a resolution that extended a massive amount of credit to Britain, for the purpose of buying military equipment. Prior to this, Britain had been running down her gold reserves to buy gear. When the gold supplies almost ran out, she bought on credit, running up a big bill. Now, **under the Lend Lease Bill**, she bought on the basis that she **migh**t never have to repay. A great deal. It was great for US industry too, because it meant that **the US government now paid for everything**, and that it simply ran up a big deficit and printed more money to parlay its way out.

This Lend Lease deal was of untold benefit to Britain. **American factories** could now pump out as much material as they could get a taker for, and have no worries about payment. **It was a goldmine for them, and salvation for Britain.**

JAPAN HITS THE HEADLINES

Early in the month, Japan continued with her moves to assert her authority in south-east Asia. She had been appointed as mediator and peace-keeper in disputes between Thailand and Indo China. This gave her licence to put military bases on their territories, sieze control of some government functions, and impose restrictions on civilian populations. She was also free to move her naval vessels in and out of their ports, and impress on them her potential to wreak havoc when called on to do so. In short, Japan was able to start undermining the two governments. This "peace-keeping" was in the best traditions of Adolf Hitler himself, who had excelled at it in 1939.

Towards the end of the month, the Japanese Foreign Minister, **Yosuke Matsuoka**, startled Australia with the statement. "I believe that **the white race must cede Oceania to the**

Asiatics. This vast territory, which is over 1,000 miles in all directions, must be made a place to which Asiatics can migrate. The region can support a population of 700,000 people. **We believe we have a natural right to migrate there**. I believe the white race **must** cede Oceania." Next day, Mr Matsuoka explained that Australia and New Zealand and the Phillipines were not part of Oceania.

The *SMH* Editorial asked some obvious questions. What areas **were** included in Oceania? Was it the islands owned by America, and European powers? Someone surely should feel uneasy. But the question remained, who should that someone be? And how did it all fit into the Japanese Co-Prosperity Scheme announced earlier? Was it all just Mr Matsuoke day-dreaming and thinking out loud, or was it a subtle way of announcing official policy? In any case, the warnings bells in Oz seemed a bit louder.

NOTIFICATION OF CASUALTIES

Australians in all the Services were now involved in direct action against enemy forces, and were being killed and maimed and injured in significant numbers. For example, about 400 men were killed in the recent Bardia conflicts. The Army authorities at home had the painful task of notifying the next of kin of the "casualty", and this was done by a simple telegram delivered to the home address. Some areas had full telegram delivery services, but others had to fall back on delivery with the normal mail (usually twice a day).

In any case, the anguish that the family felt every day, waiting for the mailman to come, can hardly be appreciated. Then, to open the telegram, and to read the gruff message, completely impersonal, was devastating. Many people seriously thought about ways of doing things better, but there were many considerations that made improvements difficult.

The Army, also deeply distressed by the starkness of the system, could do little to soften the below, and settled on the following procedure and messages. It then maintained this system till the end of the war.

Press Release. Minister for the Army, Mr Spender.

> "Military authorities are unlikely to change the method of notifying casualties by telegram. The use of ministers of religions to break the news, it is considered, would be inefficient, especially as it would require several days before a clergyman in the country could definitely report that he had delivered his message. In any case, the intrusion of a clergyman into private grief would often be resented. All telegrams would be signed with the name of the Minister for the Army."

The messages for the many and varied categories of casualty were listed. For example, they included, "severely injured", "missing in action", and "prisoner of war". They all followed the same lines. For example, for death, the message read:

> "I have to inform you that (number, name, rank) was killed in action, and convey to you the profound sympathy of the Military Board and the Minister for the Army."

Such messages appear at first glance to be heartless. Yet, there is another side to this.

> **Letters, A Mother of Sons.** The brave and beautiful Letter from Mrs Topp gives me courage to express similar views, held by myself ever since the heart-

rending subject of "breaking the news" arose, but which I had hesitated to write of, lest I should be misunderstood. Like all other mothers, I pray it will never be necessary for any bearer of bad news to call upon me, but if tragedy were to befall either of my serving sons, I, too, would prefer to receive the news alone, and to remain alone, with God the only witness and comforter of my agony for the rest of the day.

A Letter in the *Herald*, apparently from a clergyman, mentions that, in the last war, parishioners were notified that no casualties would be reported during the daytime. He states that the practice was to seek out some close friend of any war-bereaved family, and together that friend and the minister of religion would go to the bereft ones at night, when the man of the house was likely to be there. This arrangement was most undoubtedly made from kindly motives, but I hope it will never become the custom in this war. I, for one, live each day as it comes, telling myself every hour of that day that "no news is good news," and that "bad news travels fast."

Thus, if it became the practice to hold back bad news till night time, all of every future day, I (and no doubt hundreds of other women too) would be thinking: "Perhaps harm has overtaken my dear one, but they are holding the notification back," and by evening one would be verging on prostration from anxiety and distress. Again, I should hate to think that others, no matter how close as family friends, should know about, and discuss what would concern myself most of all (in my case really only myself, vitally), before I should be even aware of the sad happening. Therefore, most certainly I do believe that a telegram, straight to the point, and delivered in the usual way, is the kindlier procedure. All great grief is sacred, and should not be witnessed by any outsiders – unless those bereft should specially desire otherwise.

Comment. I suppose there is no "best" way to deliver such terrible news. And it would be wrong to think that the senders were in fact heartless. They were doubtless ordinary people who had given a lot of thought to a real problem, and who had to come up with a solution to a problem that had no solution.

HOSPITALITY FOR SOLDIERS ON LEAVE

Military personnel were occasionally given leave of a week or so. Many of them were far from home, so that usually there were thousands of lonely men roaming the streets of the cities, looking for something to do, and somewhere to go. Some of these were happy to look for the wild life, but equal numbers wanted a taste of home life. There were many womens' organizations that did their best to provide that, and their contributions to the general well-being was widely acknowledged. However, there was the occasional critical statement. Here is a response to one such.

Letters, Anne Marsh, Sydney. Statements have been made in the public press evincing resentment by a service man's wife regarding the form of hospitality that is given to the men on leave by hostesses. I am writing this to *The Sydney Morning Herald* on behalf of the great number of public-spirited and large-hearted women who comprise the personnel of the Australian Hospitality League, of which I have the honour to be the honorary organiser.

Great indignation is expressed from all who know the work accomplished among the men on leave in providing them with homes, and I have no hesitation in asserting that these women who provide this hospitality have no ulterior motives; they only desire to brighten the lot of the men who have left their homes to fight for Australia.

The charge that "the hostesses are breaking up marriages by inviting married service men to private entertainments without their wives," and that "society women, many of whom are canteen workers, are the worst offenders," is an unwarrantable and unpatriotic assertion so far as the Australian Hospitality League is concerned.

The many hundreds of letters received by us prove that lifelong friendships have been made, and among those who have expressed this appreciation are the wives of men who have been provided for. It is necessary to answer this innuendo at once so that a very false impression may be eradicated.

We are proud of the work accomplished, and the men who are married and their wives would be the first to acknowledge the inestimable benefit they have received. The thousands of unmarried servicemen we have provided with homes for the weekend and other leave would resent these imputations as much as we do. Our one sincere objective is to help the Australian sailor, soldier, and airman, protect him from possible evils to which they are liable, and to make him as happy and comfortable as we can while on leave.

NEWS AND VIEWS

Letters, Golden Rule. I direct attention to the filthy, disease-carrying habit of spitting by men? As a country visitor to the city I was disgusted with the condition of a North Shore railway carriage floor and sundry other places, including the street, and even the walls of tiled railway entrances. I shudder to think of the spread of disease and the general result if ever we were forced by war to congregate in any confined space. If offenders were heavily fined and their names published it might be a lesson to others.

Letters, Half a Pint for 5d. The introduction by Sydney publicans of a glass for the sale of beer at sixpence has vastly aroused my interest. This glass, **called a "middy," will hold 10oz of beer** – exactly half a pint. Therefore, if the Prices Commissioner has ruled that beer shall not be sold at a price exceeding 10d per pint, why is the publican allowed to charge 6d for half a pint?

As an argument against this imposition of the ULVA to extort more profit from the public let us take the case of raw milk. This milk is sold at 4d per pint. If I want only half a pint I pay 2d. Why is control so lax that the publican can get 1/- per pint for his beer when sold in these half-pint "middies"? I think that it is a matter for the Prices Commissioner to inquire into, as it appears to me to be a flagrant effort to evade the prices fixed by him.

Letters, F Walton. What a unique opportunity is presented for the display of real patriotism to those **using cars for pleasure purposes!** The urgent need for reducing the consumption of petrol is known to everyone, but an enormous quantity of it is still being used for purely pleasure purposes.

Mention was made recently of limiting the supply for pleasure cars to 3,000 miles yearly, but why should it be necessary, in these critical times, to have to resort to any form of compulsion? No compulsion has been necessary to induce the flower of our manhood to make the supreme sacrifice for the protection of their country, or for our young women to volunteer for service as nurses – not to mention many thousands of volunteers engaged in all kinds of war work. Surely the sacrifices made by all these people are immeasurably greater than would be the case if pleasure car users were **to lay up their cars while this crisis lasts!**

If the saving of the petrol now used for pleasure purposes only meant shortening the war by 24 hours, or even a quarter of that time, it would mean the saving of many precious lives.

Comment. The notion that private motorists would soon have their ration reduced proved correct. It was reduced from 4,000 to 3,000 miles per year. That is about 60 miles or 100 kilometers per week. Further, previously you could stock-pile your coupons for six months, and now this was cut two months. Bikes became popular again, but soon you could not get tyres or replacements of parts. So, you could walk or stay home.

Letters, D Sharland. I have been puzzled for a long time to know how it is that, though the public are repeatedly entreated to refrain from all gossip about the war, no similar request is made to the ferries and other steamers on the harbour, whose whistles, hoots, and cock-a-doodlings announcing the approaching departure of our troopships are certainly a form of gossip.

Up till now I have not succeeded in converting anyone in a position to act in the matter to my opinion that this custom gives undesirable publicity to military and naval secrets, and makes it far easier for the less responsible members of the community to gossip about these matters.

My hope is that the cock-a-doodlers will be asked to join the silent service.

Letters, J Blumenthal. Incendiary raids over London have proved how difficult it is to deal with fire-bombs on pitched and irregularly shaped roofs, even in the presence of watchers. The intricacies and material of most roofs are too difficult to cope with. Yet there is a method of building construction that would largely eliminate the fire hazard from direct incendiary bombs and also to a certain extent from high-explosive bombs. These dangers can largely be overcome by making it compulsory for all large buildings to be built with **a flat concrete roof with coping, sealed with compound and flooded with water**.

There are large buildings, as well as homes, in America constructed in this manner for the utilitarian purpose of sealing the roof and keeping the building cool. An incendiary bomb will splutter in water, but will be contained and made harmless, while if a high-explosive penetrated the roof and caused fire from its blast, the escaping water will help to smother the incipient flames.

MARCH: MENZIES IN THE NEWS

In Britain, from about the middle of the month, the bombings increased in fury again. London had its fair share, and coastal and country industrial centres, like Bristol and Hull, were targets as well.

Our very own Prime Minister was caught in a raid on Plymouth, as his diary entry describes.

> **...we proceeded through Bristol** (with its main shopping streets blitzed—no possible military objective) and by Bridgewater, Taunton, Exeter to Plymouth, which had a doing last night. Many ruins still smoking. Met Lady Astor at her house on the Hoe. Windows broken, and therefore sent to Admiral's Residence, after visiting a shelter for homeless and speaking there.
>
> At dinner we are warned that Hun arrives two nights running. Sure enough, just as the port arrives we are hurried into the cellars, into a corridor whose floor is some feet below ground level but whose walls are pierced by window sandbagged outside. A frightful bombing breaks out. Twice the window swings right in with the force of the blast. Twice I don my tin helmet and creep out to see the sky red with fire, to hear the sound of the planes overhead, to hear the ping of falling shrapnel, to see fires all along the city, and nearby houses and a church spire standing out as clearly as in an aquatint of moonlight.
>
> Nancy Astor and I keep the company entertained below, but the business is not really funny. The windows in the front of the house are broken. After midnight, all clear sounds...A frightful

scene. Street after street afire; furniture litters the footpaths; poor old people shocked & dazed are led along to shelter. Buildings blaze and throw out sparks like a bush fire. There are few fire appliances and firemen. Picture Melbourne blazing from Flinders to Lonsdale, from Swanston or Russell to Elizabeth Streets; with hundreds of back street houses burning as well.

Every now & then a delayed action bomb explodes (two were so close as to make me duck) or a building collapses. Millions of pounds go west in an hour. I am in a grim sense glad to have seen it. I am all for peace when it comes, but it will be a tragedy for humanity if it comes before these beasts have had their own cities ravaged. The Hun must be made to learn through his hide; for sheer brutality this kind of thing is beyond the imagining of those who have not actually witnessed it. I thought it horrible, but Billy Rootes said "Nothing compared to Coventry!!"

JAPAN QUESTIONS FOR MENZIES

Menzies, making a speech at a London luncheon, was a bit out of touch with Australian sympathies, and he was quietly pulled into line. I will leave it to the Editorial of the *SMH* to explain it all.

There is danger that certain passages in his address, which at best were not fortunately phrased, will be read as implying that waters are not really disturbed at all, and that their placidity never need be ruffled so long as all those who dwell round the ocean **behave sensibly, frankly, and in general like jolly good fellows.** He would seem to have fallen into the error of minimising the seriousness, to the bewilderment of public opinion in Australia.

Letters, E Clinton. At the present time, Mr Menzies is endeavouring to pour oil on troubled Pacific waters by making alleged “realistic approaches” in his London speeches. In effect he is saying that we have no quarrel with Japan, which indicates a leaning towards Mr Chamberlain’s policy of appeasement.

It is this very attitude on the part of the national leaders which assists the Axis to get control of such countries as Bulgaria. While it is reasonable to assume that Australians are in favour of maintaining a firm front to the Axis partners, it must be confusing and definitely harmful to the Empire cause in America when “realistic” approaches towards pacification are made in the direction of Japan by timid Australian politicians.

Comment. Menzies was not viewing Asia-Pacific events through Australian eyes. Japan was still fighting in China, and looked certain to intervene in Indo-China and Thailand. It now seemed that it was going the way that Hitler had gone, and was about to pick off small nations, one by one.

Menzies had done no real harm, except to his own reputation. Many people back in Oz were saying that he should be back here doing his job, and that he was out of touch with the local scene. This little incident gave them more ammunition, and won him no friends. He would soon need them.

HITLER DOES IT AGAIN

Hitler had some charming ways. When he wanted a country, he always asked first, and then regardless of the answer, he took it. At this time, he wanted a pathway to Greece, and only Hungary and Bulgaria and Romania and Yugoslavia stood in his way. To most people, this might have seemed quite an obstacle. But not to Hitler. He simple asked if he could trample their rights underfoot, and most of them, thrilled to be asked, agreed.

So he persuaded each of the first three nations to let him pass with promises of territories that they had always wanted, and at the same time, he had little chats with their leaders. In these, as always, he was able to mention the might of Germany and the threats she could pose to anyone who crossed her. He also mentioned special ways that the country could help him, and finished with a deadline, within a day or two, for that help to be given. At the same time, coincidentally I suppose, his troops massed on the borders of the interested nation. By this civilised method, he gained passage through the first three nations mentioned above.

Yugoslavia had strong links to Britain, and did not see the light of reason. Anyway, because of the menace of Hitler, she was at the moment having political turmoil and in fact, changing kings. So, by the end of March, she was the only fly in Hitler's ointment.

ITALY LOSES MORE NAVY

The War was once again proving to be not much fun for Mussolini. His ground troops were losing ground in East Africa, and were idling in Libya. Now, her navy took another belting from the Brits, and the remainder was securely locked again into their home ports. On top of that, her armies in Greece were losing battle after battle. Little wonder that Hitler wanted to go overland and take on the Greeks himself.

LIQUOR LAWS

The liquor laws in Oz were in bad shape. NSW was typical. Pubs were the main dispensers of alcohol, and they were almost always run-down, and grotty, and made little pretence of providing accommodation. The laws had been changed in WW1 to enforce six o'clock closing, and had never been revised. So the famous six-o'clock swill was the order of the day.

Wine was sold over the counter in wine bars and pubs, though most of it was fortified, such as sherries and ports, and was not considered suitable for drinking with meals. It was illegal to sell so-called table wines, such as riesling and claret, with meals in restaurants.

Various governments over the inter-war period had threatened or promised to fix the liquor laws, but no one was brave enough to actually do so. T**here was a church and anti-drink lobby** to satisfy on the one hand, and **a powerful hotel lobby** on the other. No politician wanted to put himself between these two forceful groups.

In NSW, the Government had once again promised to review licensing laws, but said that they would need to wait till after the War. A lot of people got excited by this, and asked why there should be any delay, but in these times, **just to say "because of the War" silenced most objectors**. But not everyone. The wine industry wanted change, and the correspondence below shows how some of them felt about the matter.

Letters, E Sheldon. Your columns have ventilated much that is absurd in our licensing laws. It is incredible that a free people should tolerate such a state of affairs.

In Australia is a great wine industry which is in difficulties owing to lack of exporting facilities. Our politicians could help this industry immediately by passing legislation allowing the sale of wines anywhere at any time with meals, the same as in any wine-producing country in Europe. Why wait till after the elections?

At lunch the other day in a restaurant (unlicensed) a bottle of icy cold sauterne was produced in a few seconds although the waiter was at pains to explain that the wine had to be fetched in from outside. The restaurateur was really bootlegging inasmuch as he sold me liquor for profit. Incidentally I was charged 7/6 for a wine which can be bought anywhere for 36/- per dozen retail.

We are allowed to drink adulterated fruit juices, gaseous soft drinks, strong tannin-laded tea, or the world's worst coffee at any time, but the juice of the grape, grown in the glorious sunshine of our country, regarding which we are prone to make much noise, is something to be rendered as unobtainable as possible as if it were a poison.

Surely no country in the world places so many unwarrantable hindrances to the marketing of its own primary product within its own country as does Australia on its very excellent wines.

Letters, V Stephen. I have been reading with interest your articles on the light wine trade, and as a grower in the Hunter River Valley I should like to add some comments from my angle. Truly one of Australia's oldest and most valuable industries is facing the danger of extinction, as already production has been reduced by more than half. The acreage of vines along the Valley is shrinking yearly. Small vineyards, some of them in the possession of the same family for two or three generations, are being abandoned and many large growers are curtailing production.

Light wines from the district have been acknowledged for the past hundred years as being among the best in the world. All the European people who drink wines drink light wines, yet here in New South Wales a valuable asset to the State as a primary industry is being completely ignored, for every outlet to the consumer is strangled.

If the Government altered the licensing laws on the following lines it would go a long way towards a solution of the problem and also encourage tourists and make the State a happier place to live in: A stricter supervision of existing licences and buildings; licences in some areas congested areas should be transferred to other dry areas; grocers' licences should be issued to approved grocers; permits be granted to restaurants to serve light wines with meals, such permits to be cancelled after inquiry of any justified complaints; light wines to be served at military canteens.

Mr Mair suggests that we should wait until the war is over. No doubt he would then say: "The war is over, you don't need a change." The war is likely to last for years, by which time this industry will be dead. We ask the public to support our very reasonable demands, and thus save our great local industry.

Letters, A Wilkinson. Hunter River winegrowers will appreciate the recent articles in the "*Herald*" regarding consumption of wine with meals, and the public support of such well-known men as Sir Norman Kater, Mr R Windeyer, KC, and Mr J F Coates. In a recent issue, Mr Coates stated that "more than half the area of the Hunter River Valley, which was devoted to the growing of wine grapes, had gone out of cultivation." What an indictment of unsympathetic legislation!

The position is tragic to those of us who knew the fine old pioneers who established the well-known vineyards of Kaludah, Cawarra, Kirkton, The Wilderness, Ivanhoe, Maluna, Mangerton, and a number of others, all of which are now extinct. Why? Can it be imagined that vineyards with the excellent reputation for quality which they had would not have been carried on by someone if the industry had been given a rational market? The fact is that distribution is so hedged round with difficulties and costs (in addition to seasonal uncertainties and risks), that winegrowers are being compelled gradually to change their occupation. This is regrettable from a national standpoint because more labour is required per acre of vines than in most agricultural occupations.

Sir Henry Manning's statement to the Legislative Council regarding wine with meals, that the

Government "would give the matter favourable consideration **after** the general election," is a reply that has been given so often that it has become unconvincing. Parliamentary representation has become a lifetime job with most members and apparently the wine industry will continue to languish unless the State Constitution is amended in the direction of limiting any member's tenure of office, thereby eliminating the element of self interest.

GERMAN SONGS IN WARTIME

Letters, Neville Cardus, Music and Cricket critic. The announcement has been made that, at the next eisteddfod to be held in Sydney, no singer will be allowed to give a German song in the German language. I argue that, **firstly**, people who wage war on poetry and words because of political reasons, or because of race hatred, simply take a leaf out of Hitler's book.

Secondly, during **WW1**, a few teachers declined to teach songs in German. After the War, their pupils found themselves at a serious disadvantage to others. No enlightened audience in London would take seriously any singer who could not sing the greatest German songs in the language proper to them. Hitler will not destroy the love of German song composers.

Thirdly, the other week, in London, a few days after one of the War's worst raids, German songs in German were sung in Queen's Hall. Also at the same concert, a work of Richard Strauss was performed. If bombed London can distinguish between Nazism on the one hand, and German music and poetry on the other, surely everyone of us in unbombed Sydney might try to follow this example of common sense.

Letters, V Webster. I agree with Mr Neville Cardus that it is extremely silly and timid to manifest any unkind feeling towards those gentle, cultured, beneficent people, the Germans, and to object to the use of their language during war-time.

What do the lives of thousands of innocent women and children or the destruction of ancient and irreplaceable buildings count for in comparison to the inestimable blessings of German symphonies and German songs, without which the world would be a barren wilderness to high-minded individuals such as Mr Cardus and myself?

Personally, I am working very hard to acquire a mastery of the German language and a repertoire of German songs, so as to be ready for the wonderful time ahead of us when German culture and the German language will permeate the earth and enable Mr Cardus to glorify their music to his heart's content.

OZ ATTITUDE TO BRITAIN

There was no doubt about the loyalty of Oz people to the British Empire, and to the King, and the Royal family. If the odd person did express some anti-British feeling, they were very quickly dropped on from a great height. In some ways, of course, this loyalty defies logic. After all, we were 12,000 miles away, and in no immediate danger. Could we not have done the same as America, and simply sent off materials at a great profit and benefit to that nation? Well, no such thought came to mind here.

It was axiomatic that if Britain was in trouble, then we were ready to do our bit. There were a few genuinely patriotic souls who wanted to help, but thought we should keep our troops **here** in case they were needed **here**. But to the vast majority, this was too remote to be concerned with. For these good folk, it might be a long way to Tipperary, but we'll **still** be right there.

NEWS AND VIEWS

Letters, Gaston Fervier. As a naturalised citizen of this country, living here irreproachably for many years, it was with bitter feelings that I read in the "*Herald*" that only **naturalised British-born** subjects shall be admitted to the volunteer Defence Corps, thus debarring the naturalised citizens of the right to participate in the eventual defence of Australia.

No other immigration country on this earth would act like this, offending and humiliating its adopted sons by an open declaration of contempt and distrust far worse yet than those already contained in the different Defence Regulations.

I dare to say with quite Australian frankness that if the inclination is persisted in to repudiate with racial conceit all those not of British birth in this country (in contradistinction to the ways of USA previously so often ridiculed as a "melting pot"), it will be soon known all over the world that the certificate of naturalisation in the eyes of born Australians is not worth the paper it is written on. All fair thinking people in Australia should know that nowadays isolation does not always turn out to be splendid.

Letters, Fair Deal. Today we have men both single and married engaged in essential industries and services who on that account are prevented from joining up by man power requirements, reserved occupation orders, and so on. It is useless having troops in the field or sailors on the ships unless they are provided with food, clothing, ammunition, and so on, and this is the job the men on the home front have to do to aid their brother soldier or sailor. Then we must have other essential services on the home front, such as water and sewerage, gas, electricity, telephones, and so on; there must be men in these services who cannot be allowed to enlist even if they are of military age.

It is high time our politicians gave some consideration and publicity to this matter, decided what is an essential service, obtained reports from employers in such services of male staff employed, and issued each man with a badge or protection certificate, without the need of medical examination. These men after the war should have extended to them the same privileges as may then be extended to returned soldiers or sailors regarding employment.

APRIL: WINSTON'S CHOOKS HOMING HOME

First of all, let me remind you that **the Oz forces in Libya** were now being **moved out of Libya** and into Greece. At the same time, Rommel was moving his army, with his beautiful Panzer tanks, **into Libya**. The Yugoslavs were just about to be invaded by Hitler, and Greece was almost exhausted by her fighting with Italy. And the German armies, backed by the Bulgarians, were sitting round at several points on various borders, licking their lips. Something had to give.

And, give it did. The situation in the Balkans turned from good to bad. On the7th, Hitler invaded Yugoslavia, and that gallant country fought bravely until the 17th, then packed it in. Also, **on the 17th, he invaded Greece.** This nation, already exhausted by its war with Italy, offered real but inadequate resistance, and was swiftly pushed back. By the middle of the month, the Germans confronted the Aussies and Kiwis. In their first face-to-face encounter with the Germans, the Aussies had two divisions, 100 tanks, and 80 aircraft.

Their enemy had 10 divisions, hundreds of tanks, and 1,000 of aircraft. There was absolutely no hope that the Aussies could stand up to this force. So, they started to retreat, followed by the Germans. As they went south, their problems grew. The Australian 7th Division, (half the **intended** forces for Greece) had their orders cancelled by the British commander in Libya, so there was no chance of relief and counter attack. The Yugoslavs pulled out, and the Greek army capitulated.

By the 25th of April, Australian troops were mustered on beaches in places like Nauplion and Kalamata, and **were evacuated,** under dive-bombing and enemy fire, **to the**

nearby island of Crete, and to Egypt. The combined force (now officially re-christened *Anzacs*) suffered about 600 dead, 900 wounded, and 4,000 captured. Six ships had also been sunk during the evacuation, and 500 men were killed there. Greece was completely over-run by Germany, and 270,000 Greek prisoners were taken, together with 100,000 Yugoslavs.

Comment. This Greek intervention was a complete disaster. No one could say it was well thought out, and well exercised. Churchill, and Menzies, both said that Imperial forces had to be sent in out of loyalty to Greece. This argument was not well received in all quarters, either in Oz or in Britain, **though given war-time censorship, criticism was muted**.

Then, the inevitable happened in Libya. The Germans unloaded their equipment and forces unopposed in the pleasant city of Tripoli, and rode off into the desert. The ANZAC force was no longer there to greet them, so with only occasional resistance, they moved all the way across Libya almost to the Libyan eastern border. At this point they paused for a while, to consolidate their supply lines. And there, more or less, they paused for months. We will return to Rommel's force later in this book.

However, in his rush to the east, he missed out on one small detail. He hurtled past a grotty little port, called Tobruk, that held the key to his push for Cairo and Egypt. It so happened that to attack Egypt, he needed supply lines, and these had to emanate from a good port. Tripoli was too far away, and the only suitable port was Tobruk. But when Rommel stopped his headlong scamper to the east, the sad fact was that Tobruk was occupied by 31,000 Imperial soldiers, including the 7th and 9th Australian Divisions.

These gentlemen seemed to enjoy the heat, the sand-storms, the underground caves, the bombings, and the various attacks on their battlelines, and showed no inclination to leave. So, there they stayed for a number of months, much to the distress of Rommel and his merry men. We will check on them in a few months.

BAD NEWS FOR BRITAIN

In Britain, the air-raids on London suddenly once again became very heavy and widespread. Not a night went past without the sirens sounding , and the bombs dropping, and the fires burning. The hospitals were full of the bleeding and dying, and the streets were littered with dead bodies. Homes and churches were destroyed, cathedrals and Parliament and Saint Pauls were blasted, and even Buckingham Palace was hit.

Over the next few weeks, raids at night occurred on coastal cities and ports, with Hitler persisting in attempts to destroy Britain's capacity to import food and materials. Some Brits saw these new attacks as heralding a determination to invade England. Some others saw them as reprisal for the bombing that Britain was now inflicting on Germany, Italy, and other nations co-operating with Germany. But Hitler wanted to starve Britain into submission, and this was one step in that process.

This was another of Hitler's silly ideas. His plans to conquer Russia had slipped a little, to June 22nd, because of Mussolini's follies in Greece. That meant that he would need every man and every piece of equipment **on the Russian front** from that date. Could he starve out Britain in by then? **No chance. A foolish thought.**

But, of course, the Brits did not know that the Russian adventure was in the offing, and just worried about the here and now. So, tension levels in Britain were raised again.

COMMENT ON GREECE AND MENZIES

Menzies, still in London, knew he was open to criticism over Greece, so he got in first with his explanations. A week before the full horror of the Greek retreat was made public in Oz, he sent off a series of messages to the Government, the Press, and the War Council. He also made a number of dinner speeches which put the London-based decisions in a good light.

He anticipated correctly that questions would be asked in three main areas. I have outlined these below, and his replies.

One. The venture ended up in very bad failure and achieved nothing. His reply was that there is always a risk with military operations. We were happy to applaud the operations in Libya that went well. Equally we should understand the distress when we fail.

Two. The operation was doomed to failure because of inadequate manpower, and planes, and tanks, and equipment and airfields. Also, the second Australian Battalion, scheduled for Greece, had not been sent. His reply was that he had not been informed of these matters, and indeed there had been assurances that the intervention was well provided for. He was not informed of the cancellation of the second Battalion until too late.

Three. The **Oz** War Council had not been given proper notice of activities and had thus not given well-informed agreements. His reply was that the War Council contained members who were not from the United Party, and thus were not Government Ministers. These outsiders had no right to classified information.

Comment. These responses were not well received back here. Even his supporters, such as the Press and members of his own Party, were lukewarm in their approval. Still, **in wartime, it is not possible to criticise Government** military policy too much. But the **grudging** support, and the emasculated criticism, told their own story. It was no help at all to the families of the men who were killed in Greece, but it was certainly true that Menzies won no friends, and lost many, from the Greek episode.

Still, people here were, in general, level-headed. The gentleman below sums up the general feeling quite well.

> **Letters, A de Barclay, Hon. Secretary, National Defence League of Australia.** It is abundantly clear to anyone who can think sanely that, as you say in a leading article, we have no time now "for merely destructive criticisms, or for re-pinings over what is past and done." Destructive criticism is one of the easiest of mental exercises – almost anybody can engage in it. How often does the destructive critic remind us of Shakespeare's line, "Most ignorant of what he's most assured"? The fact is that of all the circumstances that led up to and governed the progress of the Grecian adventure we are ignorant, and a foundation of ignorance is no sound base on which to build conclusions.
>
> Whether an initial mistake was made in withdrawing men from Libya, whether the probabilities of the Greek campaign were wrongly estimated, does

not matter now. What is obvious is that we were in honour bound to give such aid as we could to Greece when she was so ruthlessly attacked. Let anyone call our action quixotic if he like, but at least it was honourable, and to do the honourable thing is to do the right thing, even though it may be done in the wrong way.

Perhaps we had not yet fully adjusted ourselves to the terrific speed and impetus of the German mechanised onslaught; perhaps errors of judgment were made. If so, we can profit by the experience; but we will not profit by it if we allow our morale to be lowered as recriminations might tend to lower it. Let us remember Mr Churchill's warning that if we quarrel over the past, we may lose the present, and the future.

By all means let us have the fullest democratic freedom of criticism; but, above all, let us keep our heads. To quote your admirable leader again, the call is "to the Australian nation to strip itself for total war." The lads who fought in Libya and Greece and added lustre to the proud name of Anzac, would surely have it so.

NEWS FROM JAPAN

Mr Matsuoka, on his way back from visiting Mussolini, detoured to Moscow, and **signed a Neutrality Pact with Russia**. This was great news for the **militarists** in Japan, because it meant that it did not have to fear an attack from the west, and she could turn her attention to south-east Asia and the Pacific. And to the USA, if necessary. And, of course, to Australia as well. The news of this Pact **did** set some alarm bells ringing here in Oz, but given the events in Africa and Europe, once again the penny hardly dropped at all.

OZ POLITICAL AND MILITARY NEWS

The internment of aliens in Australia remained in chaos, as it had for the last year. Persons from all of those lands conquered by Germans had come here as refugees, with the Government's blessing. **Now, many were in internment camps, waiting for a chance to prove they were not dangerous spies.** Others were wanting to get **into our armed forces to serve for Australia,** but few of them had made it to date. The Letters below introduce some new thinking on this problem.

Letters, F Hafner. In New South Wales and Victoria a **great number of internees** are kept behind barbed wire on behalf of **the British Government**. Some were sent from England by error, as was revealed by a debate in the House of Commons. Although they were victims from Nazidom and classified as loyal refugees, in the first days of the threatened invasion, they were evacuated. One effect of the mistake in England was that in Australia they were accommodated under unfavourable climatic conditions. During the passage most of them lost all their property and arrived with only the things they had on them.

An official of the Home Office is making investigations in the camps. It may be presumed that they will get a fair and just deal. That would mean release and return to England or permission to go to other countries. Since only a small number of them could do so, the bulk would have to be re-transported to the United Kingdom. English authorities would be at a loss to procure shipment for such an object and to face previous problems again.

At all events, it would take the internees still a long time before they would be really free. Most of them are young chaps, some barely 16 years of age, suffering heavily under the "barbed wire complex," and, in spite of safety and humane treatments by the Australian guards, animated by the one desire of set at liberty. They would gladly prefer any work to being kept idle behind barbed wire, perhaps for years.

Is it an unreasonable thing to relieve England of her care and at the same time make use of brains and hands ready to work for the sake of Australia? A large number of the interned youths have lost all touch with their relatives, and would desire with all their heart to stay in this country, the glory of which they only know by hearsay. The Department of the Interior would have an exceptional opportunity of seeing the applicants in the flesh before considering their permits. It could take all the necessary measures to safeguard public interest by imposing conditions and stating regulations. If this cannot be done for one reason or another, let them work on farms, in factories and workshops, where hands are needed, under every control, if they apply for it. There will be no risk, but every satisfaction.

Letters, R Barnes. In the "Herald" appears a report of protest made by Mr Ward, MP, concerning the method of interning aliens. Mr Ward states that people interned are not allowed to know who has laid evidence against them, and that not even members of Parliament are given access to this information.

From accounts I have heard elsewhere, I have reason to support Mr Ward in his statement, and, although I know nothing of the particular case he quoted, I would be glad to know just how such a method – only too reminiscent of eighteenth century France's system of "letters de cachet" and of Archbishop Laud's "Court of Star Chamber" – can be reconciled with our ideas of democracy and justice. Are these two concepts to be kept strictly for our political speeches, or are they to be maintained as real principles governing our dealings with all who come under the jurisdiction of our laws – irrespective of whether they are aliens or not?

I am of the opinion that people should be interned only if they have been seen to somehow pass information to the enemy. To bury people in prison on suspicion without a single thing against them is an outrage and against everything we are fighting for.

FOREIGN LANGUAGES

The use of foreign languages, raised by Neville Cardus last month, continued to attract comment.

Letters, F Townsend. Neither the Germans nor the Italians spared or softened their contempt for English or French words used in their countries. On the omnibuses in Germany, the word "person" (licensed to carry so many persons) was struck out by authority, and the German word "volken" substituted. The word "hotel" had to be altered to "hoff," and so on. The same thing is done in Italy, and penalties for disobedience are strictly imposed.

Yet we encourage foreign words even in Sydney, viz "Delicatessen," "blitzkrieg," and so on. At best, the German language is guttural, unmusical, and non-euphonious, though rich enough in other respects. English **is admittedly a better language**, and if foreign words must be introduced they should be authoritatively anglicised.

Letters, Richard Thew. It appears to me, a war issue is being made of the question, unnecessarily. Apparently all the contributors of thought have missed the most important point – why sing in German at all in our country at any time, when we are seeking to entertain or educate a people 98 per cent of whom know no other means of expression than English?

Surely it is logical to suppose that it must be much more enjoyable, much more cultural because more intelligible and intelligent, to sing in English – even though the translation may miss some of the finer subtleties of thought on occasion, than to sing in questionable or even good German, to an audience who are hopelessly in the dark with foreign text. Ask the singer to cease singing and recite the words, and no one would listen; clearly proving that it is the musical line which holds us rather than Heine, Schiller, Goethe, Morike, etc.

All who think of these matters know that the English-speaking people are the only folk who **endure** their opera lieder, or French songs, in the original tongue. **In Paris, Wagner, Strauss, and Puccini are sung in French; in Frankfurt,** Munich, and Salzburg, Gounod, Thomas, and Verdi **are sung in German**.

PETROL WAR FUELING DEBATE

The rationing of petrol continued to get people stirred up. Below are some letters on the subject. The first two are concerned with potential wastage.

Letters, John Morton. I advised the Liquid Fuel Board, on form *COBI*, that I could manage with a reduction of nine gallons of motor spirit a month and received a letter of appreciation. The announcement, however, of a record entry for a motor racing carnival at Penrith on Easter Monday makes me think I have made a fool of myself in bothering to make out the form.

Letters, Driver. Your correspondent, Mr John Morton, should be informed that racing motorists who appear at Penrith about once a year do not use ordinary petrol.

They use "dope" of their own mixing, or else a special racing fuel that is entirely unsuitable for road machines. As none of the races are more than five miles, Mr Mort might find some consolation in the fact that, even if the racing cars used garage petrol, they would be using only a very small quantity.

Collectively, the amount of petrol used at Penrith is of an infinitesimal quantity compared with the staggering amount wasted by thousands of pleasure-seeking motorists making country tours, attending race meetings, the Show, greyhound meetings, and other functions. If Mr Morton will join me in this issue, I shall be ready to cooperate in assisting him to get to the real root of the petrol wastage question.

Comment. The Government announced that, from June, the ration for private motorists would be cut further to 2,000 miles per year, from 3,000.

The remaining three Letters deal with the saving of petrol by using alternative fuel. At various times in the past, steam-driven cars had been tried. Could they be of use now?

Letters, E Holmes. H2O's conclusion that we might be independent of petrol if the **steam car** had been concentrated on is worth analysis. At the 1900 Sydney Show, a Thomson steam car was exhibited, this being the first car to run in Australia. At the time, it appeared that steam cars were more efficient than the then petrol cars, the main objections being that it took about half an hour to get up steam to start and carrying water for long distances. However, the petrol car improved so rapidly that the steam car was soon left behind as a manufacturing proposition.

Letters, Brian Harvey. The reintroduction of steam cars, such as Stanley steamers, would not help to solve Australia's imported fuel problem, as suggested by "H2O" in the "Herald." Contrary to the general belief of the public, the steam car still depends on an imported fuel to fire the boilers, namely, kerosene or crude oil.

Letters, Hector Fraser. I have been using a Stanley single-seater commercial roadster steam car for some months now. I converted same to use coke and at the same time retained its oil burning mechanism. I can run 80 miles on a bag of coke which usually costs me 1/5 per bag. The small amount of oil used is not an item.

Apart from the running costs, a steam car is easier to ride in, faster, more durable and dependable than a petrol car. By using coke the Australian interests are directly helped. In England many cars have been converted to run on steam and the lighter cars run for as little as 1-18th of a penny per mile when using coke and use only five gallons of water for 100 miles. I agree with "H2O". Had engineers for the last 20 years concentrated on the steam car we should have had a far better car today than the best petrol car, and without all the worry about petrol.

NEWS AND VIEWS

In 1941, one way of selling daily newspapers was to have news-boys standing in the main city centres doing a brisk trade in the many editions of the Daileys. They shouted outside railway stations, bus stops, and busy streets that the world was on the brink of destruction and you can find out details for a few pence.

Letters, R Miller. I wanted to go by tram from the stop opposite the *SMH* office to teach at Daking House. This, I suppose, is quite a legitimate, ethical desire. When my eye caught sight of a vacant seat, one who should have been a lady was buying a paper from a news-vendor, who was at that time on the footboard of the tram. After waiting for the transaction to be completed, I was still on the footboard of the tram (which had started), when she decided that the paper tendered her was of an edition that she did not want. Then came the counting of almost as much change as would fill the Mint. In the meantime, my glasses were nearly swept off my face. Then, eventually, I became a legitimate tramway passenger, and was allowed to crawl into a seat.

The suggestion that I put forward is that the paper-buying public go to the news-vendors on the pavement and that the paper-sellers be not allowed on the trams at all. Some day, when we lose one of our leading citizens in this way, the practice will probably be stopped.

Letters, Norman Sheppard. I want to go on record as being one who can stand almost all the rigours that the Government is putting on us. I comply with most of the regulations, and come up grinning.

Except for the removal of bullseyes and Steam Rollers from the lolly shops. Put simply, no man can be expectsed to do a day's work down a pit, and then come up to find there are none of these to suck on.

It is a heartless Government that sets up such a system.

MAY: MENZIES BACK IN THE SADDLE

Britain had a mixed month in May. It won some, and it lost some. But on balance, it was probably a net loser. One good thing was that as the month wore on, the air raids got fewer in number and severity. Not that they stopped. Britain herself had stepped up her bombings of the Continent and even Berlin had received several pastings. Hitler thought that Britain deserved a bit of tit-for-tat, and kept his bombings going. So, the situation only improved. The bombings did not stop.

But Britain was dragged into two new areas of conflict. A gentleman called Rashid Ali, in Iraq, no doubt emboldened by Britain's defeat in Greece, staged a successful coup against the Government, and put some forces in the field. Britain felt that her oilfields there were at risk, and had to remove this menace. This took about three weeks of fighting.

Then France, under Petain, made strong noises that she would collaborate with the Germans, and that she would be likely to offer her army and navy to the German cause. In French-controlled Syria, this again posed a threat to British oil interests, so out came the guns once more, and it took a little longer to subdue these forces. Both of these actions involved large numbers of Australians, so our defence of British interests in this part of the world continued, and our casualties continued to mount noticeably.

Back in Australia, the question that was being asked in some quarters was why were Oz troops fighting in the Med and Middle East, far from Britain. Surely they enlisted to fight **to defend Britain**. The answer was, of course, that if Britain lost control of these areas, then Hitler's dream of starving her out might come true. It was a good answer, but so too was it a good question.

On the 13th of May, Westminster Abbey was severely bombed. Up till now, St Paul's roof had been penetrated by bombs, and so too had Buckingham Palace. This most recent attack seemed to be just too much, and the British Press was filled with the word "outrage". Or, more correctly, with the word "**OUTRAGE**". It was seen to be just too much to have the very centre of democracy thus attacked. From then onwards, there were more and more calls for Britain **to abandon her policy of not bombing civilian populations**. She should, argued many people, drops bombs where she wanted, and never mind who or what she hit. After all, that's what the Nazis were doing.

On the 14th, Rulolf Hess, Hitler's heir apparent, left his job, without Hitler's knowledge, and **flew himself to Britain**, and crash-landed on the property of a Lord Hamilton. His idea was that if he could intervene somehow with the power-mongers of Britain, then he might be able to stop the War in its tracks. It was seen by the Brits as a hair-brained scheme, so after they had extracted as much propaganda as they could from this freak event, they imprisoned Hess till the end of the War, when he was put on trial as a war criminal. But the event staggered and amused Britain.

After all, how many times in the middle of an enormously savage war do you have the Second-in-Command of one side enter the domain of the other side, and proffer advice on how they should behave? Hitler was not at all amused. In fact, all Hess' aides and some of his family suffered severe punishment, and the man himself was branded as mentally unstable. Hitler of course was terrified that Hess would give away Germany's plan to invade Russia on June 22. But Hess remained silent on that matter, so this grand plan was able to edge into reality without general disclosure.

Britain had some mixed news May 24th. The giant, new German battleship, the *Bismarck,* was able to parade round the Atlantic sea lanes with impunity, because of the size and range of her guns. On that date, she was challenged by two British vessels, the battleship *the Prince of Wales*, and the cruiser, the *Hood.* In a pitched battle, the *Hood* was destroyed. Of her 1,500 crew, only three survived. Britain was dismayed.

Bismarck, however, had been damaged. After a two-day cat-and-mouse game, the *Bismarck* was sunk. Her death roll was just almost as severe. Of her 2,000 men, 110 were rescued by British ships. The whole episode took less than a week, and though it ended in a British victory, once again the toll of human life was no cause for joy.

BATTLE FOR CRETE

Crete is a large island adjacent to the south of Greece. When the Australians were evacuated from Greece, many of them ended up on Crete. It seemed prudent to leave them there, because it was obvious that the Germans, once they took Greece, would want Crete as well. This was because it provided a naval base that blocked a good part of the Med, and because of the airfields there that would provide a base for air raids into Africa and the Middle East. By the time the action started, 6,500 Australian, 7,000 New Zealand, and 5,000 British troops were stationed there. But not for long. German aircraft started bombing on May 13th , and by the end of the week, these forces between them still had nil aircraft on the island to defend them.

On May 20th , thousands of German paratroops descended from the skies. By May 21st, much of the British Med fleet was destroyed off Crete. By May 26th, 3,000 fresh German troops were being airlifted in daily, to the airfields that were all held by the enemy.

For the Australians, food, water and ammunition were in short supply. The bombing and straffing were ceaseless. They had virtually no tanks. On May 27th , they were ordered to retreat, For the next three days, they were evacuated by ship, under constant air attack, during which the Royal Navy suffered terribly. Overall, Crete cost the Navy three cruisers and six destroyers, and another dozen vessels required extensive repairs. 2,000 officers of the Navy were lost at sea, and 1,000 Royal Marines.

The Australians lost 274 killed, 507 wounded, and 3,000 as prisoners-of-war. New Zealand lost 671 killed. All in just over two weeks. Crete and Greece remain unforgettable disasters in the annals of this European War.

NEWS FROM JAPAN

Japan had a quiet month, except for its war in China. One interesting report from New Zealand quoted a Chinese diplomat there saying that "Japan is exhausted, apart from her Navy, and she will not risk another war. At most, she can only help the Axis powers by creating a threat in the Pacific, and that will divert British resources away from the main conflict. Japan is not in a position to expand anywhere. She would not risk her fleet in an encounter with the US."

Dr Koo was almost completely wrong, as it turned out. But his assertion that the conflict in Europe was "the main conflict" was still dominant in Oz. Politicians and Letter-writers, and Editors still saw Japan as a potential aggressor **in company with Germany and Italy**. They held to the belief that Japan would become a **useful sidekick** if the European war extended to this region. Australia was just six months away from a major conflict with Japan, and yet there was little comprehension of this. Most eyes were still fixed earnestly on Europe, and the Middle East.

OZ NEWS AND VIEWS

Conscription was becoming a thorny issue in Oz. Some people were thoroughly exasperated with the Federal Government because they considered that Australia should be put on a full war footing. Below is a representative Letter.

> **Letters, W Mathe.** Powerful nations of yesterday are today numbered amongst the vanquished, the impossible has been accomplished, and what appears to be ruthless might and greed rides roughshod over the bodies of untold numbers of men, women and children. Are we, the people of Australia, doing all we can to right the wrong, and with this trend of thought applying all our energies to create the greatest efficiency, by filling the breaches made in our fighting units, making sufficient tools to enable our boys to complete the job; every ounce of brain capacity, energy, and united effort are needed if victory is to be ours, if our glorious land is to avoid invasion, and our women and children kept from knowing the horrors of bloodshed?

This is not the time for hesitation, delayed action by one man or woman for one day may mean the loss of a soldier, sailor, or airman. The spirit of Australia will face every danger with valour and assurance; it shrinks not from peril yet only a few have realised the true position. Let us throw off any mantle of apathy and allow the world to know that the spirit of Australia is alive and awake, ready for action in every sphere, backing up those valiant people led by unconquerable Winston Churchill along the road to ultimate victory and peace. Shall the shades of Drake, Wellington, Nelson, and the hosts of Anzacs call out in vain? Not if Australia be true to herself.

Many people who were advocating a greater war effort thought that the nation should introduce conscription of young men. **In their version**, all men of about 20 years of age would be called up, and permanently required to serve with the military until the end of the War. They **would be required to serve overseas, in conflict zones. And these would be in Europe.** This would be a big change from the present, where recruits served in the militia, for a period of about six months, and all stayed in Oz. Or they joined the AIF voluntarily, and were then potentially sent overseas to fight. The new, and very controversial elements, were the **universality**, the **compulsion**, and the **overseas service**. Let me start this discussion with a strong Letter **against conscription**.

Letters, Roger Bain. There is a lot of wild talk about conscription for overseas service. When the time comes, when we are defending **our own shores**, I will support the idea. But I remind you that at the moment we are sending our boys overseas to fight in the Middle East. They are not defending Britain at all. They are defending British commercial interests, in far-flung places. Why should our young men die to help British capitalists?

Not only that, anyone who keeps an eye on the Japanese can see that they are probably getting ready for attacks in the region here. Surely we should be preparing for this. We should be building up our own armed forces, **right here in Australia**. The idea of recruiting our boys to send them overseas to be killed is ludicrous.

Anyone can see that our army overseas is being used to save British troops from conflict. Have our leaders had anything to say on this? Should we force our boys into uniform to fight overseas without some thought from our leaders as to **why** they are fighting? If our leaders cannot or will not protect them, why should they go?

A lot of people were a lot more alarmed. Some of them were nearly hysterical. The Letters below are among the more moderate ones.

Letters, J Patrick. In today's issue of the *Herald,* I see a complaint by Sir Claude Reading about the poor support of the War Loan. I also note that there is a poor response to the recruiting drive in New South Wales.

Is it not time that someone in the War Advisory Council, or one of the leaders in the Labor or Government parties took his political life in his hands and told the people that conscription of industry and man-power is required at once, that is if we mean to retain the rights and privileges that our fathers fought for? I for one – and there are thousands like me in Australia – am ashamed of our Government's weakness. Not one Minister is willing publicly to air his views on conscription, yet surely Ministers must see how senseless it is to have our military camps crowded with young, semi-trained men and yet not be able to use them in the proper defence of Australia. Surely we all realise by now that the place to defend Australia is not **in** Australia, or are we going to be like the other smaller countries who waited until they were attacked?

I am sure that the young men of Australia are willing and ready to take their turn. I believe that everyone in Australia realises that the voluntary system is doomed, but there is a strange silence on both sides of the House about the obvious necessity for conscription. It is the fairest system, as everyone who is physically fit has to take his turn in the service of his country.

What an opportunity there is for one of our Ministers to sacrifice himself, if necessary, so long as he awakens the Government and the country to our necessity. But I feel sure that leaders who, even at this late hour, will put the country's necessities before everything else, will survive and have the confidence of the people.

Letters, Victor Segal. Whenever any attempt has been made to curtail temporarily any of our peacetime liberties and privileges, it has been said that we are fighting to prevent that very thing. Yet when we are sick, we willingly submit to the rigid discipline of the hospital or sickroom, and forfeit many of our accustomed comforts in the interests of an effective cure. Sometimes we even allow ourselves to be injected with the germs of the very disease which we are fighting.

Democracy is to us the normal healthy state. War is abnormal and a dread disease. We cannot expect to fight an abnormal condition with normal everyday weapons and methods. We are sick now with the disease of war and must discipline ourselves and forgo temporarily some of our normal rights, to overcome it. New Zealand submitted to conscription in the last war and again in this war, without permanently losing any of her democratic status. Who will say that New Zealand, controlled by what has been called a radical Labour Government, is less democratic and less free than Australia? England found it necessary to adopt conscription of wealth, resources, and manpower, almost immediately. Is our need of victory any less vital than that of England?

I will give Mr MacDonald last say on this issue.

Letters, G MacDonald. Mr Menzies will return to Australia after basking in the limelight overseas. He has an unmistakable responsibility for pushing ahead to the limit with the extensive powers he now possesses. He would be particularly ill-advised to shatter his prestige, undermine his powers, and divide the nation by reviving the old conscription question which did nothing but harm to the war effort in 1916 and 1917.

MENZIES BACK HOME SOON - AT LAST

After **four months** overseas, Prime Minister Menzies left for home. On the way he was feted in Washington, then Canada, and also in Auckland. In the Letter below, one of his fans called the faithful to give him a right royal welcome.

> **Letters, J Nightingale.** Could not a right royal welcome be given our Prime Minister, Mr Menzies, immediately he returns to Sydney? It might be arranged in the Sydney Town Hall. On the platform should be the leaders of all parties, members of the Cabinet and the War Council, and representatives of the Navy, Army, and Air Force. Thus we could demonstrate to all our unity of purpose as well as give to Mr Menzies a sincere and hearty welcome after his dangerous and extensive journeys.
>
> Few men have so much first-hand knowledge as he, and I feel sure he would give sufficient information of what he has seen to urge us all on to greater united effort. The proverb says, "a prophet is not without honour, save in his own country." But surely, we Australians are capable and broad-minded enough to do honour to such as he?

AND *HEEERE* HE IS

Menzies gave a rousing back-home speech on May 27th at the Sydney Town Hall welcome. It was full of his wonderful oratory. He talked about the greatness of the British people, "poor little street-bred people of Britain, in whose hearts burn the purest flames of courage that the world has ever known". He praised the valour of the Australian forces in the Middle East, who "spoke to me like little boys". He talked approvingly of the great Prime Minister, Churchill, who "enjoys the loyalty of the entire Parliament and the entire people, who are now concentrating on the central and imperishable things which forever must unite them."

He went on. "In one week, I saw eight large industrial centres round large factories that were turning out the materials of war. In the centres were jagged gaps where bombs had fallen. Street after street of simple homes and cottages had been blasted out of existence. Thousands of victims had been buried in common graves.

"Yet within a few days, those who were left were back in their places in the factories, smiling at their work, and working harder than ever determined to exert themselves in order that this thing should never happen to the world again."

Throughout the speech and at the end, he was loudly cheered many times, and at the end he was farewelled with many choruses of "For He's a Jolly Good Fellow." It was a grand spectacle, one that brought joy to the thousand Party faithful who attended. But outside, the news of the debacle of Crete was slowly filtering through, and many people were asking difficult questions. It would be surprising, even under the tough censorship laws prevailing, if Menzies could answer those questions simply with oratory, without giving some solid explanation of why our soldiers were sent to their deaths in such appalling circumstances.

THERE WAS NO *POLITICAL* UNITY HERE

Everyone agreed that political unity was necessary before we could marshal all of our resources for war. But there was no sign of that unity. The two Letters below, from two different camps, are typical of the large numbers of writers and commentators who bemoaned this state of affairs.

Letters, Herbert Yeates, MLA (Queensland). The statements of both Mr Curtin and Mr Forde, published in the "Herald", setting out that they were against a National Government only go to show that they are summing up the position from a party political point of view, instead of having the outlook of statesmen. If the Labor Caucus definitely decides against an all-in National non-party win-the-war Government, then I would suggest there are two alternatives.

In the first place let us admit that a proper war effort is not feasible owing to the present chaotic condition of the central Government with its small majority. Australia surely will not be satisfied to put up with this. Mr Menzies could, of course, ask the Governor-General to dissolve Parliament. Then he could go to the country, placing before the electors one straight issue – elimination of party politics and intensification of the defence and war programme by an all-party wartime administration. The response would most likely be satisfactory. However, this would distract Ministers from their proper work – the war effort.

The other alternative is, in place of a general election, a referendum could be taken to ascertain what majority of the people desire **the burial of party politics** and the employment of all available talent and energy through the formation of a National Government. Mr Curtin and his friends would find it hard to oppose such a resolution, since it would express the essence of the democratic principle that ultimately the people shall decide. And in the meantime, the important activities of Ministers controlling the war services and supplies would be uninterrupted. In such a referendum, a simple ballot paper would suffice, and there should be no need for much campaigning, because opponents of the proposal would be under crushing handicaps. The electors might be simply asked: "**Are you in favour of the elimination of party politics**, and the formation of a wartime Government drawn from all sections of the Parliament?" Only two answers could be given – "Yes" or "No".

Letters, J Ellison. Messrs Ryan and Keen have written letters advocating national political unity. These gentlemen, well-meaning as they may be, cannot escape injecting an anti-Labor virus into their appeals.

Mr Menzies's Town Hall speech was **good oratory**, no doubt. It would never, I believe, enthuse the workers of this country to the full cooperation which he expects. Not one word did he mention of the things we must see are ended with this war – unemployment, the dole, slums, the neglect of our young manhood. All these elements vital to the hope and faith of a democracy in the future were omitted in the Prime Minister's torrent of words. It may be said that the audience was enthusiastic for his national unity plea, but as I saw that audience it was composed in the main of elderly and aged persons, and not at all representative of the Labor constituency.

Mr Keen adds to his urging for a National Government an admonition of Mr Calwell and Mr

Beasley for their criticism of what is nothing short of a scandal in respect to the munitions lag in Australia. Thus he shows how honest, constructive criticism by Labor leaders is resented when once it touches the entrenched interests that view with complacence Australia's half-throttle war effort.

NOTIFICATIONS OF CASUALTIES

Letters, M. Toll. Much is being written as to the distress among relatives owing to the lack of news of those who were evacuated successfully from Greece and the non-arrival of casualty lists. As one of the mothers who, though trying to believe no news is good news, are on tenterhooks, I would like to suggest a very simple means whereby at least those whose folk were safe could have known by now. It was used by the British authorities during the last war, and was very successful.

The authorities issued to the men field cards, printed with a few phrases, such as "I am quite well", "wounded", "sick," etc and the man just addressed and crossed out the lines not relevant to his case. Thus a lot of delay in censorship was saved, weight of lengthy letters, the difficulty of getting paper and envelopes to write with was eliminated, and while not as welcome as a letter one did feel that a contact had been made.

Could not this method be adopted immediately? Even if the men were issued one field card per week, these sent air mail, would mean a regular contact.

JUNE: WHEN THIEVES FALL OUT

The aim of the censors was officially to prevent valuable information from falling into enemy hands. And the aim of various other agents of government was to keep the morale of the nation as high as could be, by sugar-coating bad events, and by exaggerating good events, by vilifying the enemy, and by any dirty or clean means that would not attract too much public attention. One result of this extensive, chaotic, and occasionally-effective system was that **any** news unfavourable to Government was kept as far as possible from general scrutiny.

This was the case with Greece and Crete. The **city** newspapers, which were under **immediate** and close censor observation, were very careful not to reveal directly details of how great the tragedy was, and to not deliberate on the failures in conception, planning and execution by our men at the top. Besides that, many of these same newspapers were supporters of the United Party, and knew that it was so precariously balanced in power that major criticism might throw it out of office. This would not have served their purpose at all.

Censorship, however, was not fully effective, and over a short time, fuller and fuller stores became available. And in the case of Greece and Crete, with this extra information there came a number of obvious and difficult questions that the Menzies administration should answer. Why were we there in the first place? Why were ANZACs the only infantry deployed in Greece? Why did we have only token aircraft cover in Greece and none in Crete? Surely it was obvious in both places that our troops were being sent to slaughter? These were the questions being asked in most houses round the nation. Menzies and Churchill were under scrutiny, and they needed real answers, not just oratory, to respond.

Critics in Britain were a lot more outspoken than they were in Oz. The conservative Press, like *The Times*, fell into line readily. The liberal Press were more outspoken. Also a number of politicians spoke up, though they were conscious all the time that there was a danger of charges of sedition if they said too much. Even **Mr Hore-Belisha**, a former Secretary of War, and a Conservative, had his criticisms heard. He complained of "the soporific propaganda aiming at covering the loss of Crete… We suffer defeat after defeat always for the same reasons, that is lack of appreciation, lack of preparation, and imperfect execution of the project. Each reverse is glossed over by the same **series of incompatible explanations**. **The narcotic of false confidence in the future** is invariably applied.

"The Germans launched the most formidable air invasion ever from aerodromes in Greece which the British authorities had previously claimed were inadequate for the RAF. The Air Ministry scorned the idea of a successful air-borne invasion of Crete, but we were ousted after an attack lasting just twelve days."

Mr Churchill replied to the criticism in the House of Commons. **Guns** were not available because at the time they were being fitted to the vessels of the Royal Navy, for their own defence. **Planes** were not available in Greece and Crete, because of the considerable distance from Britain, and the need to transport, unpack them from their crates, assemble them and test them It all took time. He went on to say that "it has been proved, time and again, throughout the war, that stubborn resistance even against heavy odds, is an essential element of victory....I much regret that the brunt of the Middle East fighting should have fell so heavily on the splendid Australian and New Zealand troops. The Germans are saying that we, Britain, **fought to the last drop of Australian and New Zealand blood.** This foul propaganda ignores the fact that it was Britain's naval forces that also suffered heavily."

Mr Menzies had a more docile Parliament and most major dailies supported the United Party. He provided, by way of answering the questions above, a homily on military tactics.

"**First**, the German is so equipped mechanically that he always moves more rapidly than we expect him to. When we work out a timetable for him, in future we must cut it in halves.

"**Second**, the Germans, operating on internal lines of operation and supply, can, so far, put into an attack anywhere, except in Great Britain, more planes than we can put into defence. To hold him in the Middle East we cannot afford to be without one aeroplane which energy, promptness, boldness, and the available means of transport can place there.

"**Third,** the bravest pilots and the best aircraft are useless without good air bases, adequately supplied and defended, and that means defence, not merely by guns but by fighting planes. It is difficult to establish such bases hastily.

"The attacking Germans surprised the defenders by the amazing and revolutionary use they made of carrier aircraft, crash landing them, sacrificing hundreds of them and thousands of soldiers in order to effect a quick invasion in force," Mr Menzies said.

"Once again the enemy's resourcefulness and speed were probably miscalculated. He is a most formidable opponent, magnificently equipped and flushed with victory, and he has been under-estimated by too many people too long."

Comment. Looking back, I detect here Mr Hore-Belisha's "**series of incompatible explanations**." In fact, though, I can't see that either of the two leaders answered any of the major questions at all.

MORE EUROPEAN NEWS. The *SMH's* Special Correspondent, on June 17th, posed a series of riddles that were bedevilling Britain. He pointed out that there had been no major air attacks on Britain for a month. There had been no German land attacks anywhere of note for almost the same period. What was going on? Were all the concentrations of German troops on the Russian border being made just to disguise some other outbreak in another location? Were troop movements reported in Belgium and Northern France evidence of another attempt to invade Britain? Was there a big build-up of troops in Libya's Bengazhi, and did that mean a renewed effort there? It really was a big riddle, and there was no one solution.

Of course, we happen to know the answer already. Or do we? We do know that Hitler had been proposing for months to **invade Russia on June 22nd**. But surely, he would not do that. Surely he would not be capable of betraying the Russian nation, this new-found friend, that he had just signed a non-aggression treaty with, and was trading so well with. Surely he did not think he could win a war with Britain on his west flank, and the might of Russia on the right. Of course he wouldn't. He would be crazy to attempt anything like that.

In Russia, Joe Stalin was convinced Hitler would not invade. For the last two weeks, he had been receiving news of troop movements, and reports from all over Europe and Japan that June 22nd was the big date for invasion. But, the normally paranoid Stalin would not entertain the thought for a moment. He refused to move his own armies into position, and he issued no alerts to the Air Force. He was completely unprepared.

So, w**hat did happen on June 22nd**? We will wait and see.

PROBLEMS WITH RECRUITING

For a few months, the number of recruits for the armed forces had fallen below expectations. Right now, this slump was continuing, and authorities were looking for reasons why. They did not have far to look.

> **Letters, H Bensley, Gilgandra.** One cannot wonder at the falling-off in the number of recruits for the AIF if a recent **recruiting rally** at Dubbo is a sample of the usual methods adopted by recruiting officers. The speaker at that gathering must have had a very poor opinion of the intelligence and patriotism of his hearers, as his main inducements were "Join up to have a good feed," "Join up to have ice cream, bacon and eggs, etc", and generally to have a good time. Also, he said that if three more would offer their services to their country, he would put on a show to entertain them; if not, the show was off. Another method of appeal was that he knew they would not let a good

chap like him down! Many of his audience were disgusted with his cheap-Jack methods.

A good, plain, unvarnished story of the objects for which this war is being waged, and the necessity for every able-bodied man of eligible age to do his bit to save the world from the domination of Hitler and his assassins, should be sufficient to induce any right-thinking eligible person to do his bit. If not, the kind of clap-trap ladled out on that afternoon would have no effect.

Letters, Kenneth Harris. It is asserted that the enlistments in New South Wales are lower than those of other States. It seems that a way must be found of overcoming complacency before the cry of "too late" rises again.

As to the method, I believe that a very powerful agent is the legitimate propaganda of those who have already experienced the Nazi "warfare." Let the nation hear from those who have been blown out of bed by the blast of a Nazi bomb, who have seen refugees crushed to pulp by Nazi tanks, and pastors and women in concentration camps lashed by Nazi youths at will. Let us have these cruel facts in all their horror. Let these descriptions of everyday occurrences be transmitted in flesh and blood broadcasts over all stations at the most advantageous times. I am convinced that such a scheme would have an enlightening effect, with a resultant stimulus to the war effort and recruiting.

Letters, Gordon Muirhead, Late AIF and Second AIF. In the spectacle of strong **he-men** performing tricks on the stage, one is almost reminded of the Felix von Luckner touch. Conscription of wealth and manpower to fight this "people's war and total war" would overcome all the "hot air" of politicians. Australians would then know that the person he rubs shoulders with is not a "cold footer," or a "wealthy profiteer," who is not prepared to defend his Empire to the "last man and the last shilling." Hitler must be fought with all the might and effort that Australia can produce. What better effort is there than national mobilisation and that, before it is too late. Voluntary effort was all right in the Boer War, not as good in the last war, and is not in the race in the present war.

Comment. There were a couple of other reasons why recruitments were down. **Firstly**, the news of the deaths and mutilation and capture of our military forces overseas was everywhere. Everyone at least knew someone who knew someone who had been involved, the papers and newsreels and radio was full of it. Church services were held, and towns and suburbs and cities all conducted civil services of remembrance. Many women went into full mourning, symbolised by black clothes and hats. My grandmother, who lost two sons at this time, went into mourning, and stayed there till she died in 1948. Many men wore black arm-bands, and men, young and old, who were inclined towards enlisting, were made to re-think. It brought home to them that death was a distinct possibility, and that the "it won't happen to me" philosophy would not protect them against modern weaponry.

Secondly, some of these men and their families were now asking what it was they were fighting for. When Britain looked to be under attack, patriotic fervour moved one hundred thousand men to enlist. But now **the action was**

moving further and further from Britain. Libya and Greece were a long way off the mark. But Iraq and Syria? These were places most people had hardly heard of. It seemed to many that our armed forces were fighting for British imperialism and oil-wells there, and correctly that they were not fighting the dreaded Hun, but the Iraqui's and the Vichy French. Would you give your life to defend British oil interests, they asked. It was little wonder that recruitment drives were floundering.

OZ NEWS AND VIEWS

Letters, Anti-Dog. Various leaders, both national and State, have drawn attention to the fact that New South Wales has still a large number of registered unemployed, and that the proportion is far higher than it is in any other part of the Commonwealth. **I suggest that one reason is the prevalence of dog racing.** I happen to reside in a large country town much addicted to "dogs". I am informed that half the dole recipients keep greyhounds. Case after case has been brought under my notice of men refusing employment because it would interfere with the training of their dogs.

At one time, local business folk rather welcomed dog meetings; now, 90 per cent, of them are bitterly hostile. I believe that, were coursing completely suppressed, at least for the duration of the war, there would be an immediate drop in the number of unemployed. A few officials might lose lucrative jobs, and a number of bookmakers would have to find a fresh outlet for their energies, but the State would benefit, and many thousands of children get considerably more to eat.

Letters, A Yeldon. The announcement that prisoners of war in Australia are to be given useful employment will be received with satisfaction. It will naturally benefit these unfortunates, both physically and mentally, to be kept occupied. The announcement continues, "the prisoners will be paid on the basis of the rates fixed by Geneva."

This portion of the announcement amazes me. I am aware that there is an international agreement controlling the welfare of war prisoners, but this **matter of payment appears to me to be going a bit too far**. No doubt, at the time these conditions were decided upon, war was waged according to the rules of cricket. I feel sure everyone will agree that war prisoners should be given the most humane treatment possible, but with the prospect of many thousands of such prisoners being sent to this country, surely the idea that these prisoners are to be paid as labourers is, to say the least, ludicrous.

WHAT HAPPENED IN EUROPE ON JUNE 22nd?

Hitler invaded Russia, that's what happened. As "brave" as it might seem, as fool-hardy as it might seem, as treacherous as it might seem, he did invade Russia. He did it in the Blitzkreig fashion, with planes, ground troops, tanks, parachutes, bombers and dive-bombers, all moving into Russia at the same time along vast lengths of the border. For the first week or so, it was a complete walkover. After all, as we saw above, the Russians had not prepared at all. It might be that Russia could gather herself and stop the awesome tide. Perhaps Russia would turn out to be Hitler's Waterloo. We will wait till later Chapters to find out.

Britain was pretty pleased with Germany's folly. She realised that there would be a huge drain on Hitler's resources, and even if he were to win a quick victory, he would be able to hold on to it only at great cost. George Bernard Shaw summed it up neatly in this Press quote:

> "Either Hitler is a bigger fool than I took him for, or he has gone completely mad. Why he believes that he can defeat Russia, I cannot imagine. The news of the war between Russia and Germany is beyond anything we could have hoped for. Yesterday Britain faced a tremendous job in smashing Hitler, with Russia looking on and smiling. To-day we have nothing to do but sit and smile while Stalin smashes Germany. Now you will see what will happen. Germany hasn't got a dog's chance."

On the other side of Europe, Japan was in a real dilemma. She had just signed a non-aggression pact with Russia, so they were supposedly good friends. She had earlier entered into the Axis Pact with Germany, and they too were good friends. What do you do when thieves fall out? Should she pitch in with Germany? Then Russia would become a threat on her western frontier. Or should she support Russia? Then if Germany continued her winning ways through the Middle East and into Asia, she would have a problem on her hands. Or, should she stay right out of the European conflict, take no sides at all, and look after herself in Asia and the Pacific?

The Japanese Government and War Cabinet went into deep discussion of this complicated situation for weeks and weeks. At the end of June, no decision had been reached, but Prime Minister Konoye did dismiss his Cabinet, though he did not appoint a new one. Also, **Foreign Minister**

Matsuoka, who recently engineered the Pact with Russia, was badly weakened. The situation remained chaotic, but the frequent mention of an **Army General called Tojo** was sending ominous signals that we should have heeded.

In Australia, all of a sudden we were confronted with the need to change our attitudes overnight. After all, for years we had **been fed the idea that Communists were dreadful people**, whose one aim was to sabotage Government and our economy though strikes and verbal subversion. If any conservative politician ever needed a scapegoat, he could always blame the Reds. In my **1940 book**, I pointed out that the Communist Party, always a target for Menzies, had been declared an illegal body, and its publications suppressed. The cry was that the Reds were not yet under our beds, but they soon would be.

But**, in a flash all of this changed.** Now, we were all on the same side, fighting a common foe. Our local **Communists, provided they beat their bosoms and swore allegiance to Australia, were now our friends**, and their opinions, suitably muted, were respectable again. Our newspapers stopped their incessant Red-bashing and allowed Communists a seat at the table again. Letters of support for Russia appeared once more in the papers.

COUPONS FOR COWS

The Government in Britain is always thinking. You need look no further than here to find evidence of this. From the London *Times*.

> The Government is introducing a scheme for rationing feeding stuffs among the different classes of farm livestock. All the foodstuffs brought into

the country must be used to the best advantage. The introduction of coupons for cows next month is intended to serve this purpose, and to ensure that dairy stock have the first call on the oil cake and other feedingstuffs that are available. Other cattle and sheep have to take second place in the war-time allocation of feedingstuffs, and pigs and poultry third place. No one will dispute the claim of the cow to priority. Fresh milk, cheese, and other dairy products from home sources will be needed in full measure to balance the diet of home-grown potatoes and oatmeal on which as the Minister for Food has warned us, we may come to rely more in the future.

The scheme for rationing animal feedingstuffs is undoubtedly complicated. Thousands of calculations will have to be made in the counties before every farmer, small-holder, and back-yarder receives his proper allocation of protein coupons and cereal coupons which will enable him to buy the feedingstuffs he requires for the different classes of livestock on the holding. But with patience and good will on all sides, the scheme can certainly be made to work and, after the inevitable creakings at the start, it should meet the needs of the time.

JULY : A CHANGE IN REPORTING

For the years **1939,** and **1940**, and the first six months of **1941**, I have started each Chapter with a discussion of the war situation as it developed in Europe. And later in the Chapter, I have looked at the consequences of this for Australia.

But now, the times they are a changin'. The war in Europe has moved far from the shores of Britain, and I can tell you that future action will largely be in Russia, the Med, and then on the continent of Europe, as the Allies sweep to victory. But not so for Australia. The Japanese at this time were just starting out on their adventures, and the nations in their path were due for a rough awakening in the next six months. And after that, for a period of worry, grief, and hardship, over the following three years.

So, from here on in this book, I have made the Asia-Pacific my prime point of entry into each Chapter, and have generally (but not completely) become more focused on that region.

PETROL RATION

For private motorists, the **yearly** ration was reduced to 2,000 miles in July. From August 1, it would be cut again, to 1,000 miles per year. Many folk at this time decided to "put up their cars for the duration". There was no petrol allowance at all for non-commercial boats.

JAPAN HAS NO OIL

Japan's Foreign Minister, Matsuoka, had always been a disruptive influence on Government. He **was a wild cannon**, inclined to make statements without Cabinet approval, make promises that would compromise his colleagues, and provoke antagonisms and raise anxieties needlessly. Without him, Cabinet became more settled, and was clearly under the controls of the pacifists.

Matsuoka had been surprised by the attack by Germany on Russia, but in true cavalier style, he had quickly decided that **his loyalty to the Axis powers outweighed anything that Russia might offer**. After all, he had signed the treaty with Russia only a few months before, and the ink was hardly dry. But he had barely a week to think about it before **Hitler asked him formally to enter the war on his side. That meant, that Japan should attack Russia.**

Matsuoka was quite ready to do this. Others in the various Cabinets and War Ministries were very much against it. They argued that, at the time, Japan had a policy to "go south" into Indo-China soon, and that it was sheer folly for it to be fighting a war with Russia in the north at the same time. **So Matsuoka had argued, threatened, sulked, and postured in vain.** Ultimately, Prime Minister Konoye dissolved his Cabinet on July 15th, and formed a new one, but this time Matsuoka was not included. From this time onwards, there was no further talk about invading Russia.

He left behind one small legacy. He had been talking for months about "going south". "Going south" included invading Indo-China. This country, made up of the Laotians, Vietnamese, and Cambodians, was on the Southern border of China, and had some desirable resources including eight air-bases that could be used to bomb the Chinese armies in south west China.

So, **the Japanese Government informed the Indo-Chinese that it would occupy their countries on July 24th**. The "request" went off to Vichy France for discussion, and on July 23rd permission was granted. The occupation went as scheduled.

America thought that this was a thinly-disguised invasion, and stopped all trade with Japan, and froze her assets in America. The British and Dutch did likewise. To the Japanese, the most concerning thing about these embargos was that all oil supplies from America and Indonesia were cut off. **Japan was left with virtually no supplies of oil at all.**

This was a major turning point in Asia-Pacific diplomacy. From here, events rolled on, and no matter what anyone did, no matter what was tried, **it is obvious now, in retrospect**, that nothing would stop the whole region from being engulfed in a major war. And that Australia, as insular as she was, would be dragged into it.

RESPONSE IN OZ

The Australian Government responded quickly. It expressed its disapproval of the Indo-China incursion by freezing all Japanese bank accounts in Australia. This did not go so far as to stop **all** trading, but it meant that all lines of credit were stopped, and the Japanese would have to pay for all goods in advance. Given the small amount of trade between the nations, the move was more symbolic that real.

Of more interest was its advances in the area of home defence. It announced in-principle agreements **to lengthen the duration of military training for the majority of young men**, and also provisions for longer terms for officers and NCO's. Again, the response was only small, and its timing delayed, but it was important in that Government was watching and was cautiously adjusting its position as situations developed.

The *SMH* posted a few Editorials that were more emphatic than they had been in the past that Japan was a danger. On July 25th , the Editor wrote:

> Japan had already secured economic domination over Indo-China. Her further demands for bases can only mean a desire to establish herself at points from which Thailand, Singapore, and the Dutch East Indies can be menaced.
>
> This is the "southward drive" in action. It will make the Japanese near neighbours of the countries which it is the avowed intention of their extremists to bring within the Greater East Asian "co-prosperity sphere." It may be difficult for Britain and the United States to do other than protest and redouble their precautions; but the dangers of allowing Japan to advance step by step, until she is ready to strike for larger gains, are obvious.
>
> Already the pending assumption by Japan of something like a "protectorate" over Indo-China has upset the delicate equilibrium in the Pacific, and the consequent increase of tension holds a warning for Australia. We cannot afford internal divisions at a moment when our security may be threatened by the march of events in our north.
>
> We have thus far remained fortunately remote from the utter destruction elsewhere. It is time for Australia to understand that these things are in jeopardy here too. It is uncertain whether the plans of our Axis enemies including Japan will allow us the leisure to introduce a war footing in this country

by painless doses, but it is to be hoped that the equipment for the five home military divisions is now becoming available. There should be no delay in implementing steps which are essential if our national defences are to be put on an adequate basis.

Comment. The general population had not as yet picked up on the threat of the Asia-Pacific developments. There were still many people talking about how our efforts to help **the Brits** were not good enough, and they were quite unconscious of the precarious situation that was developing right here.

WAR IN EUROPE

On July 3rd, ten days after the initial German attacks on Russia, German Marshall Calder was able to write in his diary that "piercing advances have been made, and over half a million prisoners have been taken, mostly in mass surrenders. It is no exaggeration to say that the campaign against Russia has been won in fourteen days, and to all intents and purposes, the Russians have lost the war."

This was not just a matter of speculation on his part. The German armies had advanced on three fronts, 1,000 miles apart, and had passed without serious challenge towards the hinterland of Russia. **On the first day of conflict, the Russians admitted to losing 1,200 aircraft.** Throughout July, results such as these continued to pour in, and it seemed that Calder's assertion of easy victory was right. "We have smashed the Russian armour and Air Force right at the beginning. They can never replace them."

Comment. Before we make a final decision on this, I suggest we wait a month or two.

RATS IN TOBRUK

The Australian troops were still holding out in Tobruk. You will remember that this small city, on the coast of Libya, was needed by the Germans to launch an attack on Egypt. But the Aussies were holed up there and, try as they might, the Germans could not dislodge them. The Royal Navy brought in supplies and re-enforcements each night, and were suffering a terrible toll in doing this.

But the Rats were sticking it out, and holding up and frustrating Rommel no end. They will still be there in a few months, so we will look in on them then.

AUSTRALIAN POLITICS

Our Prime Minister, Robert Menzies, was having a hard time of it. I will leave it to the *SMH* to point out some of the signs of this.

> It is six weeks since Mr Menzies returned to Australia, fired with the determination to make what he called the greatest effort of his life, and protesting that it was "diabolical" to have to play politics at such a time. Actually, he has been forced to "play politics" harder than ever, and the session of Parliament which was to have implemented his "prospectus for an unlimited war effort," has proved nearly barren of results. Enforced retreats by the ministry were followed on Thursday by a succession of defeats. The reverses were galling rather than serious, but they indicated how precarious is the Government's hold on the House.

> As for the retreats, they included **the delay of legislation to ban** war-time strikes and lock-outs, though the Prime Minister's prospectus only a fortnight earlier had featured a determination to prohibit such interruptions in industry. On this, Mr Menzies has had to accept Labor guidance or restraint. To add to his embarrassments, there is much disaffection among his own followers.
>
> Menzies had said "It is for us,"to make Parliament an instrument of war, and not an instrument of dissension." **At no time since its election has this Parliament less resembled an instrument of war.** Unity is lacking, and the spirit of cooperation is declining. The situation is becoming intolerable for the Administration and injurious to the national interest.

As well as the signs that his majority of two Independents was precariously balanced, he had an on-going problem. He was still much inclined to send our trained troops overseas, while John Curtin, as Labor Leader, wanted to use them for our own purposes. As time wore on, and Japan was looming as a bigger menace, Menzies' policy was getting more dubious.

CHARCOAL BURNERS

Enter the charcoal burner. Petrol was getting very scarce, so motorists were desperately looking for any alternative. With petrol burners, **dragged along at the back of a car**, the principle was that charcoal was ignited inside the burner, it slowly produced flammable gas that was piped to the engine that had been specially converted, and ignition then occurred, just the same as it did when petrol was combusted.

Obviously the beauty of cars was not much increased by the addition of these devices. They had other weaknesses. It took perhaps ten minutes of slow combustion before sufficient gas was available to drive the car. Also, in 1941, there were few places along the roadside where charcoal could be brought. So every motorist had to carry with him enough charcoal to get himself back home. Finally, they were dirty. On a day-to-day basis, they emitted smoke and dust. It was even worse when it came to removing the dead ashes.

Still, motorists had few alternatives, and the devices were generating a lot of interest and sales.

News item, July 16. Almost 2,000 persons attended a public lecture on producer gas units at the Sydney Town Hall last night. Mr C Pederick, from the Motor Traders' Association, answered questions for an hour after the conclusion of his lecture. He said that in the last year, improvements had been made in the design of the producer gas units and in charcoal for use in them.

The price of charcoal was certain to be reduced as the market expanded. At the present price, the overall cost of operating a vehicle on producer gas was about half the cost of running it on petrol.

He said that more producer gas plants and more charcoal were needed. The whole farming community could assist. Graziers with suitable timber on their land might set up kilns, which cost a little more than forty Pounds, and produce charcoal at about three Shillings per bag.

News item, July 16th. The State Cabinet yesterday considered the licensing of charcoal burners and the control of the quality of charcoal produced and sold in New South Wales.

The Premier, Mr McKell, said that legislation to enable this to be done would be submitted to Parliament early in the first session of the new Parliament. Regulations would then be issued empowering a Government authority to grant licences and to specify grades of charcoal.

The depot at Wolli Creek, the Premier said, would have a limited amount of charcoal available for delivery today. Fifty tons of charcoal a week would arrive at the depot from the country immediately, and the supply would increase as rapidly as new kilns could be manufactured and installed.

The charcoal would be available in 56lb bags at 4/- a bag, cash on delivery. There would be no credit sales.

But even back then there were conservationists on the job.

Letters, Silky Oak. Hundreds of charcoal-burning retorts will soon be erected about the country, and valuable standing trees will be cut down and slaughtered unless the authorities take definite steps to protect our forests.

All over Australia one can see thousands upon thousands of ringbarked trees and logs – standing monuments to past neglect and sheer carelessness. Are we going to repeat this appalling waste in order to run motor cars?

It has been firmly established that the highest results from charcoal are obtained from "dead" wood, i.e., trees and logs that have lain for years. Let us, therefore, use up the countless unsightly ringbarked trees and millions of logs that are such an eyesore throughout the various States – particularly on our own North Coast.

Letters, A Penfold, Curator, Technological Museum. After the last war the production of valuable by-products from the carbonisation of wood was uneconomical, because there was no market for charcoal. The present war has reversed the position. There is now an unprecedented demand for charcoal for producer gas units. So far as I can ascertain no action has been taken, nor is any action contemplated, with regard to the recovery of the valuable volatile products, some of which are indispensable raw materials for certain important industries.

Some of these industries are of value for defence purposes. It should not be difficult to recover these products in a relatively simple and efficient manner. In no other part of the world would such waste of useful products be tolerated. In view of the large number of kilns which will be erected for the production of charcoal, it does not require much imagination to visualise the enormous quantity of **valuable material which will be allowed to escape into the atmosphere**. It should be within the province of some competent authority to demand the recovery of these products.

Comment. The charcoal-burning business grew and grew. Later in the war, the burner on the back of the car was often replaced by a flat balloon on the top of the car. This was filled with combustible gas, at service stations across the nation, so that drivers did not need to carry the fuel with them.

FORTUNE TELLING IN WARTIME

Letters, A Husband. Mr Michaelis, MLA of Victoria, has drawn attention to the fad "that spiritualists, and some fortune-tellers were preying on the credulity, and grief, of women relatives of men overseas." Fortune-tellers in Sydney and suburbs do not wait for a war, but carry on their practices, both day and night, including Sunday. If these persons could be properly dealt with by our police and magistrates, there might be many less cases in the divorce court and in mental asylums.

Letters, Cliff Gray. I am angry about the number of women who are being fooled daily at a church hall near my house. These poor suffering mothers and wives and sisters and girl-friends go there to get their fortune read by the greatest charlatans in the nation. They are given misleading news that might bolster hope in the short run, but often increases the misery and despair when the true news of the men-folk come through. Cannot someone shut down these predators on human misery.

HEALTHY MIND IN HEALTHY BODY

Letters, F Jackson. At least one afternoon a week should be given to teaching the adolescent lad how to live, the care of his body, how to choose a career, citizenship, comprising his duty to his country, civic pride, municipal work, protection of birds, animals and trees, church, debates, games, and the choice of friends; art, including an appreciation of the beautiful in landscape, furniture, painting, literature, and music; the evils of intemperance, gambling, idleness, and disease; the desirability of saving money, building his own home, and some ideas about it.

In place of some of these, the adolescent girl should be taught at least the elements of domestic economy, particularly the value of foods, and the care and upbringing of children. In some restaurants in the United States, one may see the food value of the different dishes set alongside each item on the menu. Without becoming cranks, people should know at least the value of foods to their bodies, and that a tin of, say, sardines is no substitute for a grilled steak.

We should aim at reform which will help to develop healthier people, happier homes, and progressive and more beautiful towns and villages with trees, gardens, and lawns in place of ugly yards and paling fences.

Comment. This beautifully structured Letter raises five questions in my mind. **One**, how many schools round the nation came close to these ideals in 1941? **Two**, how many would come close in 2021? **Three**, if you wrote a similar Letter today, what would it say? **Four**, would the aspirations have changed? **Five,** have they stood the test of time?

AUGUST: JAPAN GETS WORRIED

Matsuoka had gone, the Americans and others had cut off supplies of fuel and other materials, and so Japan found herself in an unwelcome situation. Up till now, and for a lot of the last four years, she had been free to strut the Asian stage, sometimes talking peace, and sometimes talking war. She had actually gone to war in Korea, and Manchuria, and China, and had been talking about setting up a co-prosperity sphere, that meant subjugation for a few of her neighbours.

But her bombast came and went as control of the Government swung between the militarists and pacifists. When the militarists took control, then the knives were out. When pacifists took over, things were better. Right now in Japan, for almost three months, the pacifists were in the box seat. Prime Minister Konoye and the Emperor were fixedly pacifist, and between them they controlled the agenda **until mid October**.

The strong move to pacifism now was caused by the realisation that, given the embargoes in place, the nation had only enough fuel to last about 18 months in peace time, and less if she were at war. Konoye was quick off the mark. He summed up the situation and on August 4th, sent off a request to President Roosevelt asking for a face-to-face meeting to sort out their grave problems. He realised that there were three impediments to good relations. **The first** was the war in China. This had lost its appeal to the Japanese, and was nowadays referred to as the "China problem". **The second** was the occupation of Indo-China. **The third** was the existence of the Tripartite Treaty with Germany and Italy, that said they were mates and would help each other under some circumstances.

Konoye and the Japanese were not at all skilled in the vagaries and ineptness of western diplomacy, but they knew enough to sweeten Konoye's request with suggestion that he might give way a bit on these three issues. Cordell Hull, in Washington, was the US Secretary of State. **He thought the Japanese were an inferior race, and they were not to be trusted.** He had seen their international conduct over the last few years, and thought that Konoye's offer to talk was a stalling tactic. He expected that if everything fell right for the Japanese, they would make further attacks in Asia, and that Konoye's proposal was simply a ploy to gain time for war preparations.

So, he stalled for weeks in replying. Konoye made a further request on August 21st, and still Roosevelt had not replied. This was a lifetime for the pacifists, because now they had only 17 month's fuel left. And further, the excitable Press were calling daily for action, and the general public were getting more and more alarmed about Japan being "encircled" by the ABCD powers. That is, by America, Britain, China and the Dutch. For everyone, the clock was ticking. In seventeen months the Japanese would lose their exalted status in Asia, and become a second rate power with no bargaining chips at all.

AMERICA'S ATTITUDE

Roosevelt at times was a bit interested in Konoye's offer. But Hull continued to dampen him down. Both of these gentlemen expected that Japan might invade further countries in South East Asia, in the near future, but **no one suspected at all that there would be an attack on America herself**. And further, Hull had been asked by the US Army and Navy chiefs, to go slow and stall, so that **they** could have time to prepare for any hostilities. This was to the front of Hull's mind as he fenced with the Japanese diplomats.

In any case, as July turned into August without any response, the turmoil in the Japanese Government increased, and it gave a little ground on the three impediments as each week passed. Still, the month passed peacefully enough, and by and large, despite all the niggling from both sides, it **seemed** on balance that war could be avoided.

In terms of the European conflict, it was very unlikely that the US would ever enter **that** War. Roosevelt and his offsiders had for two years expressed sympathy with the cause of the British. Every fortnight Roosevelt gave a stirring speech threatening Hitler and proffering moral aid to the Brits. Further, huge supplies of war-making material were being sent to help out. But beyond that, in the normal course of events, the Americans were unlikely to join in.

Within the nation, there was a strong isolationist movement. The basic question for such people was why would we send our sons to fight someone else's war? We did not start it, we will give as much material support as we can produce, but we will not send our menfolk to fight it. There were, of course, many others who said Britain is fighting to preserve the values of freedom and democracy that we too uphold. We should pitch in and help them. But, the country was divided on whether to join the fray, and so the matter perpetually languished. Then there was the matter of economic realism. Under Lend Lease financing, the US economy was enjoying a grand recovery from producing materials for Britain's war. Why interfere with this?

OZ'S LITTLE SPURT

It was as if someone had rung a bell. All sorts of things happened suddenly. The Government announced surprisingly that 600,000 men were now in the Armed Services. That 56,000 people were employed in the munitions factories. That a Japanese ship, *Kasima Maru*, now leaving Oz, would be the last such ship allowed to leave, that more AIF were being sent to Malaya, and to Burma, and two large US warships visited Sydney with much pomp. Menzies told us, with Churchillian drama, that this was "our most vital hour." Curtin, and Labour stalwart Evatt, and a dozen other politicians were at the forefront, telling us that the Japanese were now ready to attack, and **some even hinted that they might attack us**. All the overseas news switched seemingly overnight from Europe to Japan and the US, and people started to talk about America's role in the war. The Oz government even requisitioned all .303 rifles from the civilian population.

Then there were the first big black-outs. All major cities had a trial black-out during the month. It lasted in each city for just half an hour, and while many people took it seriously, just as many thought it was a joke. These latter folk took no precautions in readiness for it, and simply sat it out in the dark.

Mr Hart, below, summarises most opinions.

Letters, E Hart. The last blackout test, in my opinion, was far from effective. From a high part of North Bondi, lights were frequently seen, some in buildings and others from the lighting of matches. In view of the many warnings given, this should not be, and, in the case of a raid, would quickly be replied to with bombs. It was fully five minutes after the stated time before the majority of lights were extinguished, among which were many extra bright neon signs.

The light house at South Head lit up an area of great space, and was an excellent direction post, notwithstanding that the port was closed to shipping.

We are a long way from being air-raid minded, and seem to treat test blackouts as a source of amusement. I would suggest that the Minister in charge of NES have the next blackout without warning, except at the last moment through broadcasting stations, and by way of sirens, etc. This would let the Minister know our state of preparedness and also the efficiency of the NES. It is very easy for officials to be at their posts after having been warned for weeks beforehand, but on the spur of the moment it may be a different proposition. If the time should come when Sydney is attacked from the air, the notice given will be at the most minutes, not hours.

Comment. I can remember this trial in my small country town of Abermain. It was immeasurably exciting and great fun. A few neighbours and their children were at our place, and a jolly good and noisy time was had by all. The highlight was when the warden approached, and we raised the corner of a blind. And he yelled, full-lung, "put out that bloody light." We fell over ourselves laughing for five minutes.

Second comment. The enemy threat was too far away to be taken seriously. But, the process was starting, and as time went on, the trial air raids got more and more effective.

To top all this activity, Mr Menzies thought that **he** should go back to Britain. He wanted to sit in on the British War Cabinet and put the point of view of Australia. The UAP and the Country Party were favourable to this, and so too was Labour Leader, John Curtin.

But not so the Labour Caucus. It considered that his terms of reference were too vague. Just what was he going to achieve? **Would he bring home Oz troops, and airmen, and Navy, back into the Pacific area now that we had our own threat?** He had had a chance to intervene a few months earlier, but still our boys went off to their death in Greece and Crete. Could he do better this time? Forde and Evatt even suggested strongly that **all the talk of war this month was just a war scare**, and that Menzies going overseas was just to boost his credentials as a big-time player. Beasley asked how Menzies could possibly go **if the situation was as serious as he made out**. In any case, Parliament did not approve of his going, and so he stayed at home.

CLERGY AND WAR

The clergy were under attack in some quarters. The malcontents were of the opinion that the clergy should be talking more specifically in terms of war and the terrible matters associated with it. On the other hand, most clergy and their main supporters were anxious to spread the message of God, the Biblical message of universal love of mankind, rather than hatred of the enemy we were fighting. The two Letters below present a sample of the different views.

> **Letters, T McKie.** The lack of interest shown in public worship during this time of stress and strain must be a source of concern to those who have the welfare of the churches generally at heart.

Many of the best of our manhood have already made the supreme sacrifice. Many more are waiting for the call to go overseas, among them boys who not many years ago were at school. What encouragement and help are given them from the pulpit? None that I have heard. I have seen men of the AIF attend service in Goulburn Cathedral (not a compulsory church parade), and after listening to the address, who could blame them if they never came again?

Everyone knows that they, and they alone are the men who are saving civilisation. Yet the clergy talk of the New Order and ignore the men who are making possible the founding of any New Order. What better examples of New Testament teaching could we find than the accounts of heroism and self-sacrifice appearing daily in the Press, and seldom or never referred to by the clergy? They prefer to talk of how we should spend our time on Sunday.

When the clergy are prepared to cast off their cloaks of indifference, and with them their clerical garb, and enter into the lives of the people, sharing their joys and sorrows, then, and not until them, will the Church come into its own.

Letters, F L D. As one who has never doubted the sincerity of the clergy, I think some of them have got away from "the simplicity which is Christ." Our world is rocking and we need all our spiritual strength to keep us steady and useful. Our clergy would better serve us if they turned our thoughts from war and politics to the perfect life of One who introduced the law of love whilst simply "going about doing good."

If they can teach us, their people, to follow in those blessed footsteps, we, too, may help forward the new order for "the people that do know their God shall be strong and do exploits."

CANING IN SCHOOLS

Clive Evatt, the NSW Minister for Education, was always inclined to ask for trouble, and this time he got plenty of it. **He decided to banish the cane from all State schools.** Every one who was anyone rose up in protest. All the Teachers Groups, the P and Cs, and parents and politicians were unthrilled to the core. The Letters poured in to the papers, and I summarise a few below.

Letters, Nero. Here is another angle on the vexed question of corporal punishment in schools. We have a class of decent boys from good homes. Enter several undesirables who set out deliberately to create trouble. They do not want to progress themselves, and are so anti-social as to be antagonistic to any boys who do. Speak to them, remonstrate with them, and (supported often by parents still more ignorant, anti-social, and irresponsible than they) they scoff "What do I care for her? She can't do nothin' to me."

Mastered, these fellows sometimes grow into decent citizens, but in any case the rest of the class are given a chance. Again, half a dozen or so young hooligans form in the school what they call "a gang." They commit all sorts of petty atrocities, inflict actual bodily injury (sometimes in ways too nauseous to discuss here), and terrorise the victims into silence. In mixed schools where girls are concerned, certain types of boys do not know where to stop until they bump up against the rod. But a headmaster must henceforth not be so "anti-social" as to deal with the matter in the only sensible way to deal with it. Mr Evatt says "No."

Letters, TMT. Most, if not all, headmasters use this corrective with an excellent discrimination, and the knowledge which the scholars possess that he has a cane – even though he seldom uses it – acts as a deterrent against foolish and unworthy conduct on their part. If Mr Evatt were to have some practical experience of the difficulties under which teachers are working, with crowded playgrounds and classrooms, he would surely hesitate before he made the task of exercising discipline practically impossible.

Letters, Disgusted Parent. Mr Evatt's venture into the field of pedagogy is already bearing fruit – evil fruit. My boys have attended the local school for many years. They were subjected to kindly discipline, and if they received a few blows from the cane they kept the knowledge to themselves. But what a change! Today my boy came home from school with a black eye and a contused lip. He was the victim of a big bully, who, prior to Mr Evatt's "reform," would have been too terrified of the results to assault small boys. I learn that he was detained for half an hour, and asked to write a page of lines.

Tomorrow my boy goes to a church school, where discipline is still maintained, and the weak protected against budding basher gangsters.

Letters, E Wilson, Inspector of Schools. It is not the fault of a teacher if an undesirable character enters his school for enrolment. The teacher will do his best to improve him, but if his efforts fail and it becomes a question of stern measures it is a matter for the Minister for Education, just as surely as a case of robbery, or assault, is a matter for the Minister of Justice.

Bad boys and girls in a school rob decent children of much of the benefit they are entitled to under our five million a year scheme of education. By all means, banish the cane, but arrange for the protection of teachers and studious pupils from senseless pranks of half-wits. When a boy proves himself to be a hindrance to the right conduct of a class, **he should be passed out for treatment elsewhere**.

Once parents and children know quite definitely that it is a question of **good behaviour or a reformatory,** the need for the cane will vanish.

RESERVED OCCUPATIONS

As the menfolk of the nation were being killed overseas, and a the threat of war with Japan was increasing, more pressure was being put on young men to enlist in the armed services. There was no conscription. But the pressure in some parts of the society was growing, and young men who did not want to go to war, and perhaps be killed, were not at all keen on signing up.

One dodge was to find work in a reserved occupation. For example, working in a coal mine exempted the youths from any pressure at all. In fact, such young men were **generally**

excluded from leaving the industry, and so they were freed from the contempt of some parts of society that would otherwise have criticised them.

There were many occupations that were reserved. Many parts of the Public Service was exempt, as were employees on the wharves and steel-works. The list was always changing,and individuals with personal stories were sometimes reprieved, but a reserved status helped many a young man stay out of a combative role in the war.

This was a vexatious matter for the nation, and especially for the young men themselves, and the many parents who wanted their child to be spared from war.

> **Letters, G Edgecombe.** Does it never occur to correspondents that many despised young men are employed in reserved occupations and have no choice in the matter of enlistment? Other young men of my acquaintance are supporting parents, brothers, and sisters, and their enlistment would cause extreme hardship; in fact, poverty, for their dependents. The only guide whether a man's duty lies in the fighting forces or at home must be his own conscience.

> **Letters, All In.** G Edgecombe is not convincing in his defence of young men who failed to enlist. Of course we know that there are reserved occupations, we also know that many young men make it their business to get into one of these reserved occupations. As to a man's conscience being the only guide, the trouble is that so many eligible young men have no conscience. As long as they can enjoy all the comforts of home, and a safe job, why worry? I have always said that

the only fair way is conscription. It is time the womenfolk of the ALP, together with all other fair minded citizens got together, to enforce this on the mind of the Government.

Letters, Soldier's Wife. As the wife of a soldier who, like thousands of others in the earlier days of this war, quietly enlisted without any fuss, and in due course went overseas, it is with extreme disgust that I and many of my friends in like position read of the methods now deemed necessary to induce young men to enlist and realise their responsibilities. Surely our standard must speedily be becoming lower if a variety entertainment, among other things, has to be used to stimulate the spirit we all should have if this war is to be won and the gallant men who have been through so much are to have adequate reinforcements. Those men had no bands and banners and cheering crowds to wave them on their way to enlistment.

NEWS ITEM

Two German spies were arrested within a few hours of landing on the coast of Banffshire, Scotland, recently. They were executed at Wandsworth Prison this morning. The men were Karl Theo Drueke, 35, who was born at Grebenstein, Hessen, Germany, on March 20, 1906; and Werner Heinrich Waelti, 25, who was born at Zurich, Switzerland, on December 14, 1915.

They were convicted on a charge of "conspiring and agreeing together and with other persons unknown to give assistance to the enemy and to impede the operation of his Majesty's forces, landing in the United Kingdom with intent to assist the enemy and impede the operation of his Majesty's forces, and doing an act likely to assist the enemy and prejudice public safety and the defence of the realm and the efficient prosecution of the war."

They were landed from a sea-plane off the Banffshire coast one morning. They transferred to a collapsible rubber boat, in which they took 10 hours to reach the shore. It was then dark, and the spies attempted unsuccessfully to sink the boat. Each carried a short-wave receiving and transmitting set in a suitcase, a considerably quantity of English money, a supply of food, and a revolver.

Both men spoke English and carried foreign passports.

They separated and a couple of hours later one aroused the suspicions of the clerk of a small railway station, where he was studying the timetable. In the meantime the spies' boat was found, and the search was intensified. The second man was found in Edinburgh, about 120 miles away, the same night.

When the police seized him he put his hand in his pocket in which he carried his revolver. Four other men have been executed in this country for treachery since the war began.

TWO DIFFERENT OPINIONS

Letters, Violet Fyvie Wyatt. May I discuss some questions that are exercising the minds of many women in Australia in these dark and dangerous days, particularly since the strikes in connection with two hunger-strikers. **Firstly:** About 40,000 men left their work not because they wanted to strike – the majority acted against the dictates of their conscience and their common sense – but because their self-styled leaders, unarmed save with a glib tongue, ordered them to do so. Many of those men had relatives in the fighting line, and it needed only a few to stand up to the little Hitlers and say: "We have sons and brothers at the front, and we will not let them down by going on strike," and the rest of the men would have stood by them, glad that someone had given the lead. Can it be that our Australian men are superbly and incredibly brave in battle, but have not the moral courage to stand up for themselves and their independence against these little Hitlers?

Secondly: A number of notable public women speak pleasantly and interestingly in peace times on peace subjects, but who in these war times are conspicuous by their silence. So much could have been done by women who have organising ability to further the war effort and recruiting by rallying other women of this country who are so courageous and loyal, but have not the gift of eloquence.

Thirdly: Sporting fixtures go on just the same, regardless of the life-and-death struggle that is going on across the world and threatening us closely, even at our own doors. Could not the promoters of these fixtures suspend their meetings, and forget the gate-money, for, say, one month, and so give our eligible men time to turn their attention in other and more vital directions than in those of pleasure and the making of easy money?

Letters, Nellie Quinlan. May I reply to the recent letter by Vilet Fyvie Watt? **Firstly**, what is the extent of your correspondent's association with trade unionists that she is able to say that the majority went on strike against the dictates of their conscience and their common sense. Surely, to say what 40,000 men are thinking savours of conceit.

Secondly, I am one of a family by whom trade union principles are regarded as most worthy. Trade-union-conscious men realise that a strike for a principle is on a much higher plane than a strike for an economic demand; and would your correspondent deny that the greatest of progressive reforms gained for civilisation have been attained through great struggles for principles.

As to relatives of striking men in the firing line, the wife of one striker said: "My son is abroad fighting in defence of the very thing that these men are striking for. His father and I would be ashamed if he came back and found that the things he had been fighting for had been lost at home."

Finally, does not your correspondent think that men who work at such speed as many of our men in the workshops need some little relaxation? When I see the fatigue of some of my menfolk after they have a seven-day week, or of others who work four nights overtime a week, their money does not look like "easy" money to me.

MENZIES SACKED

At the Federal elections, only a year ago, the UAP and the Nationals combined with two Independents to scrape together a majority of two. Mr Menzies, over the year, had alienated a number of his own Party, and now his attempt to go overseas, at a time of so-called crisis, for an undefined purpose, proved more than his Party could stand. At the very end of August, his Party decided that he should no longer lead it. The Country Party leader **Arthur Fadden was accepted as the new Prime Minister.**

Of course, this still left the Coalition in a very delicate position. Independent Wilson had been seriously offended during the debate on Menzies, and it appeared he might not continue to give his support. (Incidentally, the second Independent, Coles, was the founder of the Coles stores that now spread across Australia.)

The Labor Party had held its nerve now for months, and had resisted popular pressure for it to join a National Government. It had held out, expecting that the Coalition was indeed weak and would fall. Now, with the removal of Menzies, they could see that they were a little closer to their goal. Still, it would be premature to pop the champagne just yet.

....

TEN 1941 MOVIES RELEASED:

How Green Was My Valley	**Walter Pigeon**
Sergeant York	**Gary Cooper**
Hardy's Private Secretary	**Mickey Rooney**
Blossoms in the Dust	**Greer Garson**
Citizen Kane	**Orson Welles**
High Sierra	**Humphrey Bogart**
Keep 'em Flying	**Bud and Lou**
Dr Jekyll and Mr Hyde	**Spencer Tracy**
Maltese Falcon	**Humphrey Bogart**

SEPTEMBER: THE WAR CLOCK IS TICKING

All the commentators, both in Australia and overseas, thought that relations between Japan and the Allies improved a lot during September. Well, in one respect, they were quite right. And in retrospect, they were completely wrong. **Let me explain.**

In early September, when Tokyo had not heard from Roosevelt about conferencing with **Prince Konoye**, a series of internal meetings were held. As usual, some of those attending were pacifists, and the substantial minority were not. **The first decision** of those meetings, approved by the Emperor, was that Japan should continue with her efforts to find a **diplomatic** solution to her woes. She should try for a face-to-face meeting with the US President, and slowly but surely give ground on some of the impediments that were bugging the US. Hopefully, the latter would come to the party, and the oil would start to flow again. As it turned out, the Americans were making some sensible noises, and so there was indeed hope for a peaceful settlement.

Alas, however, **there was another decision from the meetings.** This was the **very secret decision to go to war on October 15th if the diplomatic efforts had not borne fruit by then.** Here we have a completely new element entering into the programme. One group, the pacifists, should pursue peace with their full vigour. The other group, led by **General Hideki Tojo**, was a War Party, and it should prepare for the start of an aggressive war in the Pacific, **and on the US**, to begin on October 15th

In Washington, Secretary of State, **Cordell Hull**, saw the efforts of the pacifists as encouraging. He was happy to see that the Japanese were getting more accommodating as the month progressed, and felt he was being successful in stalling for more time. Then, as he saw the Japanese preparations for war being stepped up, he came to **the conclusion that the Japanese were again being deceitful.** That is, he saw the Japanese as pretending to be on a peace offensive, but really getting ready for war behind the scenes. He was not at all inclined to promote serious discussions with a country that he could not trust.

So, the two countries drifted on. The US did not realise that there was now a time-bomb ready to go off on October 15th. The Japanese did not realise that their intention to make war **if negotiations were not successful** was being seen as a straight-forward determination to make war. This misunderstanding remained critical. One country said we will go to war if negotiations are not successful, but we need to make preparation for this. The other said if you make these preparations, we will not negotiate at all. It was a situation made worse by language and cultural difficulties, and by some ingrained attitudes on both sides. **The clock was still ticking.**

JAPANESE POSSIBILITIES

We should now all go on a trip, in a circle, starting from Cape York Peninsula. First, go due north, to New Guinea. Then straight up to Japan. Then go west to China, and south through that country into Indo-China and alongside those, plunge into the jungles of Thailand.

Then, we go south into the long Malayan peninsular, with the big military base of Singapore at its southern end. And from there, through all of the 6,000 islands of Indonesia (then the Dutch East Indies and other islands) back to Darwin.

Now we should review some recent events. We saw that Japan had invaded Manchuria, and China proper, and had taken possession of a great deal of territory there. Then we saw that the Japanese had "persuaded" Indo China to cede to her important rights to bases and ports in that country. We also saw that Japan now had a deadline of October 15th and that if negotiations with the US failed, it was very likely that she would unleash her military forces by land and sea and air, onto various parts of Asia and the Pacific.

We will keep this map in mind as we proceed.

AUSTRALIANS IN MALAYA

Australia had been becoming increasingly wary of Japan's intentions over the last few months, and had gradually, by dribs and drabs, been building up her forces in Malaya and Singapore. These troops were slowly being trained in jungle warfare, but they had little else to do, and nowhere to go. Below are a few news items emanating from this army.

> **News item, Sept 1st.** Australian troops and officers in Malaya resent the recent Army decision here to issue the Australian slouch hat to all **Imperial** troops serving in the Peninsular.
>
> The Australians regard the slouch hat as their own possession, and a definite identification tag, of which they are just as proud as the Scots of their glengarries and the Indians of their turbans.
>
> It is understood that the decision to issue slouch hats was taken because of the shortage of pith helmets. The order affects Malayan volunteers,

some of whom are already wearing slouch hats, Britishers, and Indians, including Sikhs, who cannot be persuaded to wear steel helmets.

An English brigade major whom I met in northern Malaya was wearing an Australian hat. He said he was not waiting for the general issue, but had bought one.

Some Australians suggest that the issue of emu feathers, like those of the Light Horse in the last war, would help to retain their identity and individuality.

OTHER MILITARY IN MALAYA

The message was getting through that there was a need for military forces in Asia, as well as in Europe and the Middle East. So Press reports showed a steady increase in the numbers going to Malaya and Singapore.

News item, Sept 4th. Further strong reinforcements of Indian troops have arrived in Malaya. They included seasoned infantry recently serving on the north-west frontier of India. The troops are fully equipped with the latest weapons, proved in the Middle East. It is reported that the men are fit, hard, highly trained, natural mountaineers, well versed in jungle warfare, and confident of their ability to deal with any enemy likely to be met.

A British artillery contingent which accompanied the Indians is equipped with the latest weapons and tractors. An Indian signal unit brought a wireless set designed for jungle use. All the units are fully mechanised with vehicles of the latest design. Ancillary units are included to meet every contingency.

News item Sept 9th. Large numbers of the latest type of long-nose Bristol Blenheim bomber have reached the Far East, to reinforce the RAF. Malaya is now receiving men and material from Britain, Australia, and New Zealand, and material from the United States.

A communiqué issued today states that the long-nose Blenheim has been successfully used in large numbers over industrial Germany as well as over the invasion ports of the Low Countries and Norway.

The Blenheim, it says, bore the brunt of the Allied counter-attack during the Battle of France. Day after day these planes harassed the enemy's advance, bombing troop columns and mechanised units, blowing up bridges, and blocking roads.

News item, 12th Sept. The suggestion that the Australian Minister for the Army, Mr Spender, might visit Singapore has focussed attention on a number of legitimate complaints by the AIF in Malaya. Grousings are part and parcel of the lifc of any fighting force fit and keen for action and disappointed that it has not seen any. Investigation generally shows that much of the criticism is unfounded, and also that the opinions of individuals often are not shared by the majority.

Nevertheless, there are three legitimate complaints awaiting attention. They are:

Anti-malarial equipment, which can be manufactured in Australia, is vital for troops in jungle country. When the troops bivouac, special squads should spray the jungle and swamps. Men who volunteer for service to guard Australia's "back door" certainly are entitled to the fullest protection against malaria. The necessity of keeping the forces in first-class health also is obvious.

Uniforms are being supplied from British India. They are badly tailored, and, in consequence, they chafe and cut the wearers' bodies. Clothing for forces stationed in such countries as Malaya needs special attention. Men on manoeuvres and on long route marches in steaming heat need the maximum degree of comfort provided by tropical clothing.

The need for better entertainment by a permanent body of entertainers is vigorously taken up in the AIF journal published in Malaya. It suggests that a dozen thoroughly versatile entertainers, drawn from any of the units, should work full-time as a quasi-professional troupe to provide the backbone of regular shows.

The AIF Journal says that a real and widespread need exists for the entertainment of Australians in Malaya, and suggests the formation of a special unit drawn from all other units. "Waiting to fight is a strain, and fighting is a strain," states the *AIF Journal.* "Our state of mind depends to a degree on the mental recreation provided. Organised entertainment is as important as organised sport, and it must necessarily be self-entertainment."

Comment. Our military and political leaders were keen to preserve the fiction that army life was all milk and honey.

I bet you that the writer of the above piece would never have got it past the censor if he had not put in that first grovelling paragraph.

EVENTS IN EUROPE

Britain enjoyed a good month in September. The air raids were getting fewer and fewer, and instead the RAF was pounding away at enemy targets with great enthusiasm. The Battle of the Atlantic was showing better results, and the unofficial intervention of the Americans from bases in Iceland kept a large area of the Atlantic more or less free from the German submarines. The fact that winter was getting close meant that even the biggest alarmist could safely reckon that there could be no invasion of Britain until spring, and so that much-hyped threat was fast disappearing. Britain itself was safe for months, though her men-folk in combat areas were still faced with terrible dangers.

The Germans had made good progress in Russia. The three prongs of her attack had won easy victories, and she was many hundreds of miles inside Russia on all fronts. Her progress had inevitably slowed as she stretched her lines of supply, and as she had more and more captured territory to control. But her march to glory was not at all impeded, and Adolf was reportedly most loquacious and relaxed round the dinner table. He was fully confident that victory in the east would be won within a few months, possibly before Christmas.

NEWS AND VIEWS FROM OZ

Reform of divorce laws. Politicians throughout the nation regarded changes to divorce laws as too hot to touch. Despite persistent cries from the populace, there was a strong reluctance from church-fearing State politicians to even discuss this matter. At the moment, all such legislators were saying that there would be no changes because of the War, and hoping that they would be then excused.

But still the Letters kept coming through. These two below sum up the position of persons who were married to persons who were insane. Of course, this was a small part of the population that wanted other reforms, but it would not be until the Whitlam Government of the early 1970's that substantial changes became effective.

Letters, H D B. You report that the State Government will not proceed with divorce reform now, and possibly not for the whole three years of its office. I plead the cause of those silent sufferers who must wait on until **insanity is made a ground for divorce** in New South Wales. Is this so much to ask? Today, inside mental hospitals, provided by the State, are many utterly incurable mental patients.

Some of them stand in the legal relation of wife or husband to normal, healthy, and sane folk in the community. Willing and often able to support the afflicted partner to the best of their ability, it is natural that some of the normal folk wish their freedom, to live again, perhaps in happier, more fortunate marriages; it is natural that they desire to move among men and women, seeking their company unembarrassed.

But, as the law stands, they are trapped. The law condemns them to patience without respite, and refuses them the love and affection which many could find in a possible new helpmate, denies them marriage, home, children – and what courage it takes a man or woman to wait on and on, in the hope that one day the simple unimpeachable justice of their claim is recognised, that incurable insanity is a ground for divorce.

Today the State Government works in the difficult milieu of wartime; yet to insert insanity as a ground for divorce is the ideal type of work which can still be done by the State. Such a law **would not divert one man from the war effort**, nor use one ounce of material.

Letters, V W H. As observers of more progressive and humane marriage codes abroad, we find the present apathy to divorce reform in New South Wales hard to understand. Some oppose reform in the hope that the incurable may be cured. Surely no sane community would legislate to ensure the suffering of many of its citizens here and now on the mere chance of a patient being cured in the indefinite future – especially when medical knowledge holds that such a chance cannot occur.

Were the impossible to happen and a cure take place, might we not reasonably expect the cured person – if not devoid of all human understanding – to condone an act of re-marriage if such had taken place?

Others hold that marriage laws are immutable. But history shows that every human institution has changed, however tardily, in response to man's changing environment and knowledge. Opposition to reform comes chiefly from those who say that marriage laws should be immutable.

But the desirability of establishing any law rests on this consideration: Does the law add more to than it takes away from human welfare? By making incurable insanity a ground for divorce, the welfare of no one is lessened, but the welfare of many is increased. Only an ignorant conservatism, or a sadism that rejoices in the torture of fellow citizens, would deny this.

Apart from the question of desirability of reform, one may query whether the time is opportune. In this regard, a former correspondent pointed out that such legislation would in no wise hinder our war effort. The present Government that, in seeking to abolish capital punishment, reveals such a sympathetic attitude to the malefactors of our community, should display a like compassion to those of our law-abiding citizens who, if not faced with capital punishment, are, in regard to one vital aspect of their life, confronted by a living death with the insane.

OZ PRODUCTION OF MUNITIONS

Newspapers were reporting the large number of hours being worked, and the stress that it was placing on families and persons.

Below is a typical comment made up from three newspapers who commented on this growing problem. I point out that none of these papers was generally sympathetic to the industrial claims of workers, so that the supportive tone of the Editorials becomes more convincing.

Composite Editorial, Sept 7th. It is largely a sign of the times that disputes and stoppages in industry should have been occurring with disturbing frequency as the war becomes prolonged. The stress of production, and the need to constantly adjust to new machines is placing greater strains on willing workers than we can expect them to bear.

The industrial machine is now being driven at a pace to try human endurance, producing fatigue and irritation. Adjustments are constantly being made in classifications of labour and rewards for skill, and fatigue is perhaps the underlying reason for the impatience with which some claims have been pressed. At the outset of the war, men possessed of special skill and experience were called on to work excessively long hours in order to keep the wheels of munitions industries turning. Twelve-hour shifts have been unavoidable, but if they are maintained too long, they lead to a sharply falling output.

No man can be expected to simply turnout each day for work, and do his shift, then come home to sleep, and get up the next morning and repeat all that. That is what is being demanded by some people. Provision must be made for recreation, whether it is recreation at sports or the races or the movies. Of whether it is just sitting in a chair and reading a book, or looking into the fire.

Unless we make such provisions, the stress level tearing some families apart will increase. The fact that the number of industrial accidents has doubled since last year suggests that the strain is telling. The men at the front are not our only heroes. We should recognise that the men in munitions factories are heroes as well.

NO STOCKINGS? NO WEDDING DRESSES?

Things were getting really serious. In a typical wedding of 1941, Austerity was the order of the day, and the wedding dress was very simple, and not made of the customary first grade silk.

Letters, A G W. With the freezing of all Japanese assets in this country and the consequent disruption of trade relations, there must come about a serious problem with regard to silk yarn. It is possible that a small quantity is available from China, but in the present unsettled state of things in that country it can only be a very small amount in comparison with Australia's normal requirements. As large quantities of silk are used in the manufacture of parachutes for the Air Force, it would appear to be an essential war material, and, as such, should be placed under Government control, even if this involved the **prohibition of its use in the manufacture of wedding dresses and stockings**.

With regard to the latter commodity, there is, I believe, a **good substitute for real silk** manufactured in USA, **called Nylon**. It might be possible to manufacture this yarn in Australia under licence, or, if that is not practicable, the yarn in its manufactured state might be imported in order to conserve supplies of silk yarn.

Letters, B R O. The establishment of nylon manufacturing in Australia would need a tremendous investment and the process is controlled by patents which are the property of the American Du Pont Company. Manufacturers in Australia have naturally made every effort to secure nylon yarn, but have been so far completely unsuccessful.

Comment. The problem of wedding dresses was later solved by using silk parachutes. These became available, at a price, through the black market, once American troops came to Australia in numbers.

NEWS AND VIEWS

Every now and then I have to remind myself that Oz still had its share of **non-military** problems.

Letters, H K W. The State Government proposes, and the Tariff Board recommends the Federal Government, to make inquiries with a view to the better marketing and distribution of fish. Would it not be as well to ascertain first whether fish are available in sufficient quantity to satisfy the needs of the people? My interpretation of a broadcast by Professor Dakin of the Sydney University, a few Sundays ago, is that he doubts whether there are, on the Australian coast, fish in the quantities found and captured off the European coasts.

If netting is allowed in the estuaries along our coast, the result will be that the nurseries of the fish will be destroyed and next year we shall be in the same position as we are said to be today. If fish are to be supplied to the people in substitution for meat meals regularly, say, twice a week, it can only be from the deep sea. Estuarine supplies would not be sufficient.

Letters, AUSTRALIAN. The closing of the Australian market to overseas-made hurricane lanterns has created a situation whereby people are compelled to pay over the counter the exorbitant price of twelve Shillings each. The pre-war price for the American lantern was five Shillings. Why this audacious profiteering?

News item, Sept 20th. The NSW Chief Secretary, Mr Baddeley, will make inquiries into a report that about 800 pigeons were killed or maimed in a pigeon shoot held at Gunnedah on Sunday. Mr Baddeley said, in the Legislative Assembly yesterday, he would ascertain whether a licence had been issued for the shoot, and would see if in future pigeon shooters could not be compelled to use clay pigeons.

Mr Tonge (Lab., Canterbury) asked the Minister: "Is it a fact that scores of these unfortunate birds were slaughtered on Sunday by alleged sportsmen of sordid minds and low intellect? Will some of these birds die a lingering death in the fields, and will the Minister immediately amend the Birds and Animals Act to give the pigeons the protection to which **their work in peace and war-time entitles them**?"

OCTOBER: ABANDON HOPE, PACIFISTS

Diplomats in America and Japan really earned their keep this month. Not that they had much to show for it, because at the end they were not able to point to anything major that had been concluded. The whole Asia-Pacific issue was still up in the air. America perhaps thought that she had forced some further concessions out of Japan, and she was right about that. For example, Japan was sometimes talking about quitting the Axis powers, and sometimes about leaving China in 25 years. But these were only baits for negotiation, and the Japanese Cabinet was not at all committed to such moves. So, as the month wore on, the US tightened the screws, and Japan was one month closer to a petrol drought.

In Japan, one major event had major repercussions. When October 15th came round, and there had been no diplomatic breakthrough, the militarists demanded that Prince Konoye should keep his promise, and launch attacks on the chosen targets. Konoye, and his backers, would not do this, but that involved such a loss of face that Konoye was forced to resign as Prime Minister. War Minister Tojo was chosen as his replacement, and it might seem that it was now certain that Japan would soon go to war.

However, the Emperor stepped in. He had strong pacifist leanings, and he influenced the new Cabinet to once again adopt the policy of seeking to negotiate, and at the same time, prepare for war. We have heard this before, six weeks ago, but this time, the power in Government had swung to the warriors, and it was only the influence of the Emperor that was keeping them at bay. There could be no doubt this time that if negotiations failed, war was a certainty.

In the US, Cordell Hull knew only a little of this. He had no idea that America would be the first target, so he just kept stalling.

So, once again, at the end of the month, the time bomb was ticking. But this time, it was down to its very last fuse.

EVENTS IN RUSSIA

The Russians were taking a hiding. On the central front, the Germans had moved to within sight of Moscow. On the southern front, they had captured Kiev and were making good progress into the Caucasus. In both of these areas, the outlooks were uncertain. **Perhaps Russia would indeed collapse, and where would that leave the Allies? Surely, Hitler would then turn around, and once more attack England.** Perhaps, the British should heed the voices of a small minority of persons who were calling for the use of British troops on the eastern front, to help the Russians. There were even a few pundits who wanted Britain to attack Germany via France, by an invasion, and so divert the Germans away from the west. But that was far too ambitious at this stage. So Britain waited.

Perhaps Russia could stem the tide. She certainly had the man-power to do that. Also, perhaps, like Napoleon, the winter would come to Russia's aid. Even Hitler could scarcely expect his troops to advance in minus thirty degrees. So that war went on. The losses were being counted in millions of men on both sides. It was a disaster that had no discernable end date.

THE OZ ATTITUDE TO RUSSIA

Australians were very uneasy about our new cozyness with Russia. This is hardly surprising. Over the last two years, we had watched in disgust as that nation had attacked Poland, and taken away one third of her territory. A few months later, we had watched in anguish as little Finland had been bludgeoned into submission by that giant. Then, that same giant had thrown its lot in with the Axis powers.

On top of that, for a decade and more, Australians had been taught by every authority in the nation that Communism and Russia were irretrievably linked. Russia was Communism, and Communism was Russia. Only a year ago, all strikes in this nation were supposedly caused by the Reds, who were taking their orders from Russia, and who were intent on subverting production to bring this nation to its knees. At the same time, we had declared the Communist Party illegal, had taken its money and property, had closed its newspapers, and persecuted its officials.

Now that it had swapped sides in the European War, everything had supposedly changed. Now our wonderful propaganda machine was regaling us with stories of Russian heroism, and Russian gallantry, and Russian nobleness of purpose. Naturally, we still opposed Communism, but that was just a small political difference. We should no longer see the battle between Communism and Capitalism as important, but rather concentrate on how important it was that Russia hold out against the Germans and ultimately defeat them.

Of course, this latter attitude was the only sensible one, and no one should deride that. But for many an ordinary citizen, the about-face in attitudes was too much to stomach, and his new love for Russia was restrained by long-held feelings of fear and contempt of Communism.

This pragmatic attitude was summed up by the first Letter-writer below. And the willingness to help was presented by the second. The third on religion, struck a chord with many persons. It was regarded as a commonplace that religion was suppressed in Russia, and all the Churches were violently opposed to Communism. So, again, the large body of people who believed this had problems in adjusting their attitudes.

Letters, F E M. Canon. A Garnsey appears to have let his well-known human sympathies run away with his head and also to have forgotten many things in wondering why orthodox Labour objects to its adherents associating with the Australia Soviet Friendship League. It has been clear for a long time that Official Labour is opposed to Sovietism, to the Soviet political organization, and to the subversive and white-anting tactics of the "Friends". It should never be forgotten that the "Friends" were silent when Russia joined with Germany in carving up Poland (and so starting the world war), also when Russia attacked Finland, and again when Russia occupied Bessarabia. Until Russia was herself attacked, the "Friends" said the war was an imperialistic war. The foregoing is not to say that we should not give Russia all the aid in our power, as exhorted by Mr Churchill.

Letters, J Forsyth. The Spartan defence of National and Democratic rights now being fought by our Russian ally calls for the utmost aid being given as urgently as possible, not only from the humanitarian point of view, but also the preservation of the freedom of the British Commonwealth of Nations which is so bound up with the battles being fought on the Eastern War Front.

Australians admire the stubborn fighting of our Russian ally, forgetting all political prejudice and bitterness, and desire to render every assistance possible. Excellent work is being organised by the Russian Medical Aid, and Friendship to Russia Executives, but may I – who have had practical experience of the Russian armed forces – suggest immediate steps be taken to arrange for the manufacture and supply of **sheepskin coats** for winter wear by the troops. I cannot stress how necessary these coats are, and I do hope that immediate steps be taken to arrange for their supply.

Could we not arrange a joint committee of graziers, and Russian Medical Aid committees and Aid and Friendship to Russia Executive to further this object? I am prepared to give my practical knowledge to assist the design and manufacture of them. I am sure, if funds are not available in Australia, the Russian Government will purchase them, or even make available credits through the Government of the United Kingdom.

Letters, O Fleck. Two different radio commentators this week, Mr J A McCallum and Mr John Dease, have, in commenting on religion in Russia, suggested that all is well with the Church in that country. Mr McCallum seemed to see but one difference between the Church in Russia and that in Christian countries, and that was in the attitude of the leaders of the nations towards recognition of the Church. Mr Dease quoted Russian authority to the effect that Russia permits freedom of religious worship and freedom of anti-religious propaganda, and he seemed to imply that these words assured the Church of a similar freedom to that which she enjoys here.

The fact is that the Churches in Russia are but tolerated, and they are permitted to do no more than conduct their services (if their buildings have not been taken away from them). Clergy are not permitted to seek to bring people to Christ or to church. Bibles may not be printed or imported. Parish papers, booklets, handbills, radio, and all other means of spreading the faith are forbidden. The Church may not prepare young men for the Holy ministry, and she may not bring in clergy from other countries.

On the other hand, the anti-God societies have the use of propaganda. You tell of the closing of two anti-religious newspapers owing to the shortage of newsprint. The opponents of religion have all the power of a great nation at their command that they may injure and discredit religion, while the Church is refused the right of reply and the right of appeal. In plain words, the Church is crippled in her ministry. By all means let us give every support to our splendid ally Russia, and pray for the Soviet, too, but let us also keep a balanced mind, and remember that Marxian Communism can never tolerate religion – the one must destroy the other.

Comment. The remaining three Letters convey the ambiguity felt by the writers. Keep in mind, though, that these were Letters published by daily Newspapers, who were constrained to publish thoughts that were not too critical of government policy. I can tell you, though, from talking to hundreds of oldies, that in the privacy of their own homes, people were much less circumspect, and the general opinion was that the sins of the past would not be readily forgiven.

Letters, R Pert. Many correspondents writing on this subject have failed to realise that whether the Soviet allows religious freedom as we know it, or not, is of little concern to the great mass of the people, who have come to link the Church with a past and darker age.

Those who would allow religious prejudice to rule their reason and prevent them from extending sympathy and aid to Russia are playing into Hitler's hand, for it is obvious that he believed by drawing the Soviet into the war, he would divide the British people, and so weaken the Empire before making the final attack.

Letters, A Bridges, Sydney. The Russians are not fighting for us, but for themselves. But they are fighting our enemies. Therefore, the plea to aid the Russians by contributions and comfort is logical.

However, local Communists should not be suffered to exploit the position as an opportunity to boost Bolshevism. Up to the time Germany invaded the Soviet, Reds in this country inveighed against and sabotaged the war effort. Their subterranean methods are still manifested in strikes, particularly in war industries.

Letters, Fair Deal. As one, who at every opportunity year in and year out, in private and on public platform, denounced Communism but who, since Russia became the enemy of Hitlerism and established indisputable claims to the support and interest of every Britisher, I wish to register a feeling of disgust at the seeming apathy displayed by thousands of those who, in a variety of ways, promenaded the safe pavements of this city quite oblivious to what the day stood for. This day had been reserved in Sydney as a special day to give Aid to Russia, via a button appeal.

Everywhere, thousands stalked our protected paths minus a sixpenny badge, and plus an air of supreme indifference, levity, and complacency. In a well-known restaurant where I lunched, not two per cent wore a badge, and to see the jovial demeanour of those who at least **could** spend sixpence in return for what the courageous Russians are doing for them, made one extremely depressed.

Perhaps it needs a few air raids on Sydney to bring many thousands to a realisation of what is being done on their behalf by countless thousands whose lives are sacrificed week by week overseas.

Comment. People remained diffident about Russia right throughout the War. Indeed, leaping ahead into 1948 and thereabouts, it came as a great relief when the Russians officially returned to their former policies of outrageous conduct, and we as a nation felt justified in fearing and hating them again.

NATIONAL APATHY

A fair segment of the public were always saying, monotonously, that the Oz attitude towards the War was apathetic. They were able to point to the fact that many men, particularly the young, were not serving overseas. They were able to say that strikes were lowering the nation's production. They also complained about the numbers of cars outside golf clubs, clearly indicating that people were using their rations for selfish reasons at the weekend. The "apathetic" argued back, sometimes giving reasons for this and that, and sometimes asking the accuser what they knew about the matter, and mostly shrugging and saying "silly old biddy".

But it was true that right now, the Australian people were indeed very apathetic towards the looming Japanese crisis. Granted we had increased our military presence in the Pacific, and that out munitions factories were working their men to the point of exhaustion, and that we were now producing many of our own planes and guns and ammunition. To that extent, we were miles better off than we had been a year ago.

However, **public awareness of our very serious situation simply had not dawned. Still**, in the face of the war clouds gathering around us, we had not tumbled to the reality of the disastrous consequences that were looming.

The Letter below looks at how **our own propaganda machine had contributed to that attitude of "she'll be right".** In a long Letter, that summarises the arguments of half a dozen lesser correspondents, he presents the following analysis.

Letters, Dr Frank Louat, Constitutional Association of NSW. There appears to be a belief among us, unspoken but very generally held, that however far this war spreads it will pass by the shores of this country like a far-off storm. The peoples of nation after nation, which Hitler has struck down, cherished the same belief until the thunder of the cannonade shattered their illusions. We have our chance now to profit by the experience of others, but it seems that we have not yet learned the lesson.

The Australian picture is one of politicians manoeuvring for power, of business men grumbling about taxation of dividends, of workers holding up industries for an advance slice of the new order that will never come unless we win. It is disturbing to realise that for the next three weeks the contest for the Melbourne Cup will bulk almost as largely in national thought as the struggle for Moscow.

The public can hardly be blamed for this state of mind. It is **the fault of our whole system of propaganda**, which ever since the war began has been busy proving elaborately that there is nothing to worry about. Our radio News Services dismiss a Nazi advance of 50 miles in 50 words and fill up the rest of the time with reports of trivial successes. The war commentators, who write and speak for us, are in many cases irrepressible optimists, who are forever detecting blunders in the enemy's strategy, dwelling on his difficulties, and minimising his victories. We are encouraged to lose ourselves in admiration of the scale of our present war effort instead of measuring the vast further effort needed to win.

There may be other peoples who need to have this kind of anaesthetic administered to them to prevent panic, but it is not needed in any British country. The first condition of getting national unity and a full war effort is to tell the people the position without any varnish. In spite of all the comfortable assurances of propagandists, there is a current of uneasiness in public opinion which needs only a plain exposure of the facts to be expressed in action.

If, in spite of their magnificent resistance, the Russians are overwhelmed, the war will move at once to a new and more serious stage. The breaking off of the Japanese-American diplomatic talks, which seems to be imminent, may confront us with a grimly altered situation in the Pacific.

The public is **not** being prepared for these happenings by anything that is being told to them. Our war publicity methods have not changed since the British people were encouraged to rejoice in the impregnability of the Maginot line. There seems to be a feeling on the part of those in authority that to admit the bare possibility that we might lose this war would strike a blow at public morale. There is every reason to think that the exact contrary is the case. There is all the difference in the world between realism and defeatism.

Letters, Ralph Doyley. I most heartily endorse all Dr Louat says, and would go further and say that the initial mistake occurred on the night of the momentous day when war broke out, and our then Prime Minister, Mr Menzies, made a powerful appeal to the public all over Australia to observe the policy of "business as usual". A faithful observance of that policy by the great mass of the people in our country has, I am sure, been largely responsible for the detached and apathetic attitude the public generally have towards the gravity of the present war situation.

CHANGE OF GOVERNMENT.

In early October, the inevitable happened. In the Federal House of Representatives, the two Independents decided not to support the Coalition in future, and **so Labor was given the task of running the country. That meant that John Curtin became Prime Minister**.

DIETITIANS ON THE MENU

Letters, MB, MRCS, Eng., DPH, Sydney. I find myself unimpressed by a correspondent's glowing remarks recently about those hospitals "fortunate enough to possess a fully qualified dietitian," who sweepingly states that "in no department...has there been more improvement." Granted even that the dietitian is well versed in "calories" and "vitamins" and has more than a mere superficial knowledge of physiology and anatomy, two vital questions arise: Can she cook? Will she cook?

Is she able to herself perform the actual boiling, baking, frying, etc., and, if so, can she demean herself to such prosaic details? May it be that in many cases most of the "menial" work is superciliously delegated to "inferiors"? As a medical man with first hand experience, I have evidence that there is something much amiss with just this "fortunate" type of hospital. Tasteless, unappetising food might be expected from an ardent pseudo-scientific dietitian, but a rice pudding whose surface was burned and whose interior contained absolutely uncooked rice grains would be a reflection on the ability of even a mediocre housewife, and might be a fatal dish for certain gastric cases. The facts suggest that it might be better to drop high sounding titles and replace dietitians and their holy of holies – their "laboratory" – with a cook and a kitchen.

Letters, Nurse. I am a senior nurse in a large city hospital. Ours is one of those "fortunate" hospitals equipped with dietitians. They are absolutely superfluous.

Since the dietitians took over the control of all food departments, things have been getting steadily worse. Much of the food served both to patients and staff is so unpalatable that it is uneatable and so a terrific amount of waste goes on. When the trays are sent from the kitchen we are often ashamed to deliver them. It does not need a BSc degree to enable a person to realise a sick person wants something tempting, not a great slab of half-raw steak, for instance.

Granted that the scientific study of food values is becoming increasingly valuable in the prevention and cure of illness, the fact remains that the science is very much overdone. The proper place for dietitians is in their laboratories doing research work, not meddling and muddling in things that are outside their domain.

The growing army of dietitians is squeezing itself in to a profession already overcrowded with specialists and expanding by usurping the work formerly done by doctors, nurses, cooks and social service people. Keep them out of the kitchen, and give us a few good cooks!

Letters, P D. I should like to protest on behalf of the overworked, underpaid, fully-qualified dietitians. Dietitians must be capable of superintending all cooking in hospitals, therefore they must be able to cook. To expect hem actually to do the cooking is as ludicrous as expecting a surgeon to sterilise his own instruments during an operation. Nurses are there for that purpose, just as cooks are in the kitchens for cooking. The dietitians would simply not have the time for it, however willing.

Of course, there are good and bad dietitians just as there are good and bad doctors. But to condemn all because of an alleged burned rice pudding is as unfair as to condemn all doctors because of a single wrong diagnosis.

With these criticisms against the dietetic profession, it is not be wondered at that students, after obtaining their science degree, are chary of taking on a course giving them long hours – longer than nurses' hours – poor pay, and non-cooperation of, not say kicks from, the brother profession.

Regarding the complaints of the sister profession it can only be said that, nurses have not yet been educated to understand and appreciate correct cooking. Among other things, they still demand overcooked vegetables, all vitamins and mineral salts destroyed by soda, and, what is hard to understand, still encourage patients to rebel against foods that will help their cure. To the sister who says she is ashamed to serve what is sent to the wards, I would suggest that she makes her complaints, not to the newspapers, but to the chief dietitian at the training school where she is situated.

PETROL RATIONING

Letters, Walter Thompson, Lismore. I cannot agree that "all country towns are faced with stagnation and bankruptcy" as a result of the unfair petrol rationing. This morning I counted 366 motor vehicles parked in the main business block of Lismore.

Letters, Anti-idiots, Redfern. Mr Thompson of Tamworth should be told that the motorists are parked in Lismore because they do not have the petrol to drive home. They will be parked there till they get their next 20-mile ration next month.

News Item. Motorists who pool their petrol for a trip to Melbourne for the Cup will be liable to a fine of 100 Pounds and imprisonment for six months. The acting General Secretary of the NRMA, Mr H Richards, explained that a ration is issued only for a specified vehicle. In reply to a query, the State Liquid Fuel Control Board pointed out that the pooling of rations for use in one car was an infringement of National Security Regulations and was punishable.

Letters, Common Sense, Paddington. The ban on petrol pooling is about the last word in bone-headed and unimaginative departmental control. With the small allowance that various people have nowadays it is impossible for them to do other than small and futile journeys, in fact, barely enough to keep the battery alive. Surely when a few friends can pool their tickets and take their annual leave in places especially adapted for that purpose no harm is done to the State as no more petrol would be used than is allowed.

STOP PRESS

The Army has announced that the Rats were being withdrawn from Tobruk. The troops were going to several destinations. A few would return to Australia, while the bulk would go to Asia-Pacific zones such as Burma, Malaya and Singapore. Their places in Tobruk were taken by forces from Britain and the Empire.

****

10 HIT SONGS FROM AMERICA:

Chattenooga Choo Choo	**Glen Miller**
Boogie Woogie Bugle Boy	**Andrews Sisters**
Elmer's Tune	**Glenn Miller**
Song of the Volga Boatsmen	**Glenn Miller**
Don't Want World on Fire	**Ink Spots**
I Hear a Rhapsody	**Jimmy Dorsey**
Yes Indeed	**Tommy Dorsey**
You Made Me Love You	**Harry James**
All That Meat and No Potatoes	**Fats Waller**
I'll Be there in Blossom Time	**Andrews Sisters**

NOVEMBER: ON THE ASIA-PACIFIC BRINK

Many years ago, as a young man, I studied a subject called "Education" at Sydney University. Part of the course dealt with the learning phases that two-year-old children pass through, and one of these was "parallel play". That was a time when two or more young people would sit together, and play with the same toys, but would not play **together**, or communicate with each other.

During November, Japan and the US engaged in such play. Diplomats from both countries talked and messaged, leaders, Prime Ministers and Generals and Admirals from both sides and in between, had their say, the Press in half a dozen countries felt they had something to offer, and the President and Emperor, each knowing half the story, dabbled or did not dabble as they saw fit. But, with all this activity, only a few certainties emerged.

One was that the Americans were playing for time, and thought that Japan would not attack anywhere. Certainty, it never entered their head it was **they** who would suffer the first onslaught. **Another** was that Japan would wait only till the end of November for diplomatic activity to produce success, and then she would go to war, without any further if's and but's.

So, diplomatic activity was very high. In mid November, the Japanese sent a special diplomat called Kurusu to Washington to try to pin the US down. The response, at last, was that the US demanded that Japan should quit the Axis agreement, and move its troops out of China and Indo-China. Japan had already promised to make some minor concessions on these matters, and wanted to know what else she had to do. **Cordell Hull** came back on the 28th with the strange demand that Japan should behave in a peaceful manner, and agree to a three-month non-agression truce towards all nations.

That was it, as far as Japan was concerned. She saw that the US was simply stalling for time, until Japan was out of petrol, and while the US built up its own forces. She wanted some agreements on action **now**, and this new demand was, to her, simply maintaining the status quo for three more months. And then presumably, the parallel play could start again.

From November, the die was cast. Over the next few days, Japan continued with her parallel play, but at the same time moved her troops and ships and planes into position, ready to attack. She sent off a large fleet into the Aleutians, outside the range of American reconnaissance aircraft, and by December 7th, had them in position near Pearl Harbour, ready to go.

No matter what anyone did, it was too late. **War in the Asia-Pacific was now certain.**

EVENTS IN EUROPE

The Russian armies, on all three fronts, were suffering severely. The toll was tremendous. Russia at this stage admitted to over one million, and the numbers were increasing by 50,000 every day. But there was a ray of hope for the Russians and Allies. **Winter had come a few weeks early**. This meant that the ground had turned to mud, and to ice soon thereafter, and made it difficult for Hitler's tanks to move forward. Also, the fogs kept his planes out of the air. On top of that, the Germans were not equipped for cold weather because, when you think about it, the Barbarossa invasion had been planned to start on **June 22nd .** It had been **delayed for six weeks** while Greece and Crete were attended to. **This delay, a gross strategic mistake, now was reaping its reward.** The German advance faltered in the face of the extreme Russian weather, and it seemed that Hitler's troops might not have such a merry Christmas after all.

In England, the Battle of the Atlantic was going a lot better, with the sinking of fewer British ships. As well as that, for the third time in a year, the Italian navy was given a severe belting, and was just about out of the War in the Mediterranean. Then there was more good news in that British and Empire forces were attempting to break out from their foothold in Tobruk, and looked likely to gain control of Libya again. Australians by now were fully evacuated.

Still, all was not perfect. The UK **aircraft carrier**, *the Ark Royal*, was sunk, with only one life lost, on the 14th. Then sombrely, the Government announce that 29,000 ground troops from Britain had been casualties of war since the beginning, and that Australian casualties were 13,145. Royal Navy figures were as bad, as were those of the Royal Marines.

Comment. "Casualties" included men who died, or were so seriously injured that they would not be able to return to the Services. They also included Missing, and Prisoners of War. The British Government came under fire from many quarters when the figures were announced. **Australia's losses were way out of proportion**, and charges were levelled that the **Aussies had been used as cannon fodder in Greece and Crete,** while the Brits had been spared.

Churchill maintained that the losses in the Royal Navy and RAF, which were mainly British, showed that Britain had not shirked her duty. In Australia, censorship presented mainly the Churchill line, **but in ordinary Australian households, comment was bitter.**

Winston Churchill had some good news for Australia. On November 11th, he uttered another grand speech in which he promised Australia and the "Far East" that Britain was on the point of sending a substantial fleet to Singapore, for the defence of the region. In fact, two massive vessels were already on the way. This was clearly in response to the tension in US-Japan relations, and was to be seen as a warning to the Japanese that Britain too would be involved if a war broke out.

Churchill went on to say that Britain would also give to Russia 550 combat planes over the coming months. This gift was gratefully received no doubt, but there were many people in **this** region who criticised it one month later when **Singapore had few planes available for its defence.**

REACTIONS IN AUSTRALIA

Early in November, **a German admira**l, Leutzow, **urged Japan on radio to attack Australia**. Several Australian politicians spoke out in reply over the next few days. The Prime Minister, Mr Curtin, claimed that Australia "was well prepared to resist aggression. A year ago German propaganda suggested that Britain could not protect herself against aggression. The German warlords know better now. **The Japanese will learn a similar lesson if they attack Australia.**"

He claimed that "large numbers of German agents and propagandists have been installed in Japan, and have tried to insinuate into the minds of the Japanese people the notion that the European war gives them the opportunity to follow Italy's example and stab democracies in the back. The Federal Government has been aware for a long time that Germany has been desperately endeavouring to compel Japan to enter the war on the side of the Axis.

"All this is bad enough. But Admiral Luetzow's broadcast is the first occasion on which the Germans have had the unparalleled impudence to issue a public invitation to Japan to attack this country.

"The Japanese will not be taken in by such crude and naïve propaganda. Their national pride must compel them to repudiate the idea that they can be made the tool of Germany in her attempt to dominate the world by force. The rest of Luetzow's vapourings show that he knows nothing of Australia's resources, of its history, of its traditions, or the temper of the people. **The invitation to Japan to invade us is nothing short of an invitation to Japan to commit national suicide."**

The Minister for the Navy, Mr Makin, said that the Navy was ready to meet any emergency. The Service was in a state of absolute preparedness, and would exercise every diligence in preserving the integrity of the continent and its adjacent possessions. The Minister for the Army, Mr Forde, said that Australian defence preparations, carried out over a number of years, were nearing completion. He assured the people of Australia that the country's preparedness was increasing daily.

Letters, Wilfred Wenborn, Sydney. Dr Louat recently took Australia to task for complacency germinated in the political attitude that the public must not be upset. **What better example of this attitude could there be than in the official comments to the Luetzow tirade?** "We are well prepared," states Mr Curtin. Only the test of battle will prove that statement. We heard it before about England, but the mercy of Providence spared England at a time we now know she was anything but prepared. What more fatuous prattle could there be than in the comment, "The Japanese will not be taken in by such crude and naïve propaganda." Could not Luetzow's speech have been used by politicians to urge that we be something more than "well prepared?"

At the time of Munich I pleaded in a letter to the "Herald" that "we build no fool's edifice." One wonders if that building is now not nearly complete in some quarters in Australia, and that it will only be demolished by enemy bombs falling in Martin Place or Canberra.

Comment. I think these comments fit extremely well into the comments made last month by Doctor Louat. You will remember he said that Australians were fed statements that assured us that everything was under control. The gentlemen (above) making those statements were all in privileged positions and knew, or should have known, that everything was not hunky dory. But they poured out these utterances that patted Australians on the head, and then stuck our chests out and talked about **Japanese national suicide if they attacked us.**

The real facts were that Japan had a population of 160 million people, and we had one of 7 million. We had a coastline of 12,000 miles to defend, and negligible Air Force and Navy. Our Army was one twentieth the size of Japan's, and most of ours had only basic training. If these gentlemen **had** to reply, they could have alerted us to these facts, instead of giving us the guff about "no problem, mate."

Little wonder, when it was so obvious that their statements were blatant propaganda, that sensible Australians took little notice of these men on these matters. The **unanswered** question was where could they get reliable information from?

THOMAS BLAMEY'S VIEW

Thomas Blamey was Australia's highest ranked soldier. He had been with the Australia troops in Cairo, and Egypt. He had seen them in their victories in Libya, and had been on the last plane out of Greece. He had returned to Australia for a brief period, and had the following words to add to the discussion about Australia's readiness.

News item. Blamey's views.

I have had a look at the Australian way of life, and now I want to get away from it. To speak candidly, it sickens me. We are living in a fools' paradise. Everything out here shows a spirit of carnival. When will Australia realise that we are right up against it, that we must fight or perish?

The falling-off now of reinforcements for the AIF means that, in the inevitable campaign **next spring**, our AIF abroad might not be as effective as it could be. That is a very serious thing. Australians seem to be ready to pay for the war, but not ready to fight. The men of the AIF abroad and in Tobruk resent this sort of thing. They are staggered at the strikes that take place, and they feel keenly that fellows who are getting three times the money, and are taking no risks, are being looked upon as wonderful heroes for making shells.

There is an idea in Australia that if you make equipment you need not send away any men to fight. There is something wrong somewhere. When will Australia wake up?

Comment. Even this distinguished soldier was missing the point. **Obvious now to us,** at this time the danger to this nation was from Japan. But his thoughts were still about Australia in the Middle East, and about the war emanating from Britain. It seems **our leaders** somehow had their minds fixed on anything but the menace that was now so close.

PUBLIC OPINION ON READINESS

The Australian population, though kept in the dark, were smart enough to know that, as a nation, we were getting deeper and deeper into trouble. Many of them thought the solution was to recruit more soldiers, and that conscription was the way to go. The Papers were full of Letters on the subject.

Letters, G Leibius, Sydney. If we are not blind to the fate of country after country in Europe – the safest and probably the only way in which to win the war is also to devote to war purposes, either directly or indirectly, so far as it may reasonably be possible to do so, the whole of our man-power, and the whole of our woman-power: in other words, to organise total war, as out enemies have done – or, in the words today of General Sir Thomas Blamey, to "pull all possible weight." This implies, of course, an end to the chaotic system under which, in a life and death struggle, a nation depends for its fighting force in the decisive theatres of war solely on volunteers.

For the wars of past times this answered well enough; but it is clearly not enough in a war against a great nation which, for years has prepared and organised to win the mastery of the world, and is using the whole of its immense population to achieve that end. Democracy has its duties as well as its privileges; and the defending of one's country is surely both a duty and a privilege. For us, as Democrats, conscription of wealth and man-power should long since have become a national slogan.

In a democracy, conscription is no longer merely to save an aristocratic and moneyed class, leaving the masses in the same condition as before, but to save democracy itself and all that it has won during the ages, and holds dear, and all that it hopes to win still; and the "time-lag" of democracy in Australia in still failing to recognise this is simply appalling, and, under present world conditions of "total war", a menace not only to the national safety, but even to the national existence.

Letters, One Australian Citizen, Muswellbrook. I wonder how many other Australians listened with amazement to one part of Mr Forde's speech on Tuesday morning, when he said, in effect: "If the required reinforcements are not forthcoming, then Australia and the people shall go into extinction forever."

Apparently, sooner than see conscription brought in, these leaders of our country would see their own land and everything they hold dear exterminated!

What men are these who govern us? And what is to become of our lads overseas? Are they to be left stranded without help?

Not one soul to whom I have spoken of conscription is against conscription. In fact, lots of young men would welcome it. They say it would be far easier for them – and those in power – and each man would be put to the job best suited to his ability.

Letters, Esther Roland. I am a person who has done nothing whatever to help the war effort. I'm by no means unique. The majority of Australians are just like me, and General Sir Thomas Blamey was rightly "sickened." I have not bought a War Savings Certificate, and if I could afford a war loan, I've no doubt I wouldn't, anyway. I have not restricted my spending on luxury goods as Mr Curtin asked. In fact the war has made absolutely no difference to my life except to make certain commodities scarcer and dearer.

But I'm not a hopeless case. I believe in this war. I was deeply disappointed in Mr Curtin, of whom I was a supporter, when **he revealed his horror of the very word "compulsory."** I have come to the conclusion that not one of our leaders can really believe the war is worth winning – otherwise they would make the winning of it compulsory. Therefore, as one of that majority who will not restrict their spending, subscribe to war loans, or enlist, while the "other fellow" is not doing likewise, I earnestly look for a nationwide petition to Parliament for conscription of wealth and manpower alike.

Letters, A Hillier. Our Government should have the courage to follow in the footsteps of New Zealand Labour, and introduce conscription, so that every man will be thoroughly trained and able to take his part in defending this country where and when he is most required.

Comment. All of these writers were actually flogging a dead horse. They were thinking in terms of the European war. But the folly of Greece and Crete, and the oft-perceived absurdity of protecting British oil companies in the Middle East, had **silenced the patriotic drum there**. But the call for conscription continued to be a strong one, and it remains to be seen next year whether John Curtin, who hated the word "compulsion", ever heeded that call.

AMERICA'S ATTITUDE TO WAR

The US and Japan were alike in at least one respect. They had pro-war groups and anti-war groups. In America, the President and the State Department had been inclined to support the British from the very beginning of the War. Over time, in the last two years, their desire to help Britain had increased greatly, and now they were providing finance and weapons and planes at a great rate. But no man-power was forthcoming. Their problem was that they were faced with a large number of anti-war advocates, who opposed war perhaps because they had seen no benefits from participation in WW1. **Or** because they did not want to see American lads sent overseas to be killed in someone else's war. **Or** they were happy with the prosperity that was coming from providing war materials for other nations to use. They were dozens of different reasons. In any case, they collectively formed a lobby that prevented the US from entering the fray. Had she done so, the nation would have been terribly divided.

The same attitude was apparent, more or less, to a war with Japan. No one wanted that. If America was called on to play the role of policeman somewhere in Asia or the Pacific, then so be it. Most people accepted it as America's role. But the thought of a full-scale war was anathema to them; they just did not see it happening.

Comment. To take this forward as a comment, I do not think that America, if she had not been attacked, would have **ever** entered the War, either against Germany or Japan. There is no blame attached to this. Just that people, sensible and well-meaning people, saw things differently, and fortunately had the right to say so and be heard.

OZ ATTITUDE TO WAR WITH JAPAN

Over the last two years, Australia had transformed itself. Back in September 1939, we had virtually no Armed Services, no munitions or arms industry, we had no concept of making our own planes. Now, we had completely changed that, and had close to a million people, men and women, in uniforms of all sorts. In reaching this point, progress had been frustrating, and it seemed that every step forward was matched by one back. But, it turned out, the ratio was **two** forward to **one** back , and the net change was enormous. Of course, had we had an authoritarian type of government, had we had a Hitler at the helm, we would have achieved much more. But as it fortunately was, the progress was almost miraculous.

The people though, were the laggards in this process of change. In their attitude to war, **they had been kept**

uninformed, and their heads had been filled with nonsense. The popular conception was that the Japanese were quaint, though warlike, they were hopelessly inefficient, their planes were slow, they had no worthwhile navy, and their army was a joke. They couldn't even speak English.

Then there was the furphy that "while we have Singapore, we are safe". This base was somehow supposed to protect the Pacific, from one corner to the other. And then there was Britain. If Japan displayed any real aggression, Britain would dispatch its Navy, and troops, and send them packing. **In retrospect**, it was a thoroughly fanciful world that would completely collapse over the next months, and leave Australia bewildered, fearful, and, as it turned out, united and determined.

THE KILLING FIELDS

In writing *this Series of books*, when I come near the finish, I sometimes get off the fence I have been sitting on, and talk about something that has been getting to me throughout the many months of writing. I want to do that now, in the middle of the night. If, when you come to this read this part of *this book,* you find a blank page, you will know that, in the cold light of day, I have scrapped the item, and thought you would be better off with a blank page instead.

So, in a philosophical vein, I am turning **to deaths in this dreadful War**. **First of all**, I am referring to military deaths. Not deaths of civilians, nor am I counting the maimed and crippled and disfigured, nor those who were permanently missing. Nor the psychologically damaged. Just what is termed "military deaths". The number of such deaths for

Australia, over the entire War, was 30,000. Britain and the US each suffered about 350,000.

Secondly, I want to talk here about Russian deaths, not just the 10 million servicemen killed. Russia also had 13 million citizens killed. These were part of a population of 170 million. That is, one person in every seven was killed. Many of them died through enemy fire and bombs. Many of them froze to death. Many of those who froze were shuffling aimlessly along country roads, in vast hordes, trying to get away, to nowhere, from the war. All of them were from families, mums and dads and kids, just like the families in Australia. What they wanted was to be left alone, to make some sort of living, and to sleep in their own beds in their own homes.

But …**they were slaughtered instead.** As I write, I read of the victories that the Russians win in the next few months, and I understand their jubilation, but I cannot at the moment shake off the enormous feeling of despondency, that mankind can have any part in creating such calamities. I know that it is all in the past, I know I am suffering a let-down that comes with finishing a book, I know I will feel better in the cold light of the morning, but now, as the tears creep down my cheeks, I feel despondent, exasperated, miserable, heart-rent, dis-believing, overwhelmed, fed up, tormented, and frustrated to the point of desperation. Apart from that, you will be pleased to know, I have never felt better.

DECEMBER: TORA TORA TORA

Russia had a great month in December. It started with victories in all of the major areas that saw the German advances stopped in their tracks. As the month progressed, the Russians gained back some of the ground that they had lost, and devastated the German forces, and siezed huge quantities of armaments. After that, in the New Year, both armies froze in position, but when the fighting re-started, the Russians took up from where they had left off, and steadily pushed the Germans back. The Huns were not out of it completely, and made counter attacks, in the region of Leningrad and the Caucasus, but these petered out, and by Christmas of 1942, **the Germans were facing a complete defeat on the western fron**t.

Without giving away too much of next year's story, I point out that this was, of course, a huge relief to the Allies. Every time throughout the War that Hitler tried to fight on two fronts at once, he messed up. The fact that he was pre-occupied on the western front for so long debilitated his forces elsewhere, and meant, for example, that Rommel in Libya did not get the support he needed, and so again, by Christmas 1942, Hitler's hopes of capturing Egypt and the Suez were slim indeed.

At the same time, in December 1941, the Battle of the Atlantic continued to give better results. So, it seemed that the Brits **might** have a better Christmas.

Comment. Over a year ago, Finland had been under attack from Russia. This little nation put up a magnificent defence that forced the Russians away over winter, and it succumbed only in spring. At the time the whole world admired and extolled Finland, and that same world mourned when the Russians occupied and punished her.

Now, under German influence, she was frustrating Britain's attempts to help the Russians. So Britain declared war on Finland. From peacock to feather duster in no time at all.

A BAD START FOR AUSTRALIA

On December 1st, it was announced that the Australian cruiser, *HMAS Sydney*, was missing and presumably lost in battle. She lost a complement of 645 officers and men. The location of the battle was not revealed at the time, but was later stated to be off the Western Australian coast at Carnarvon. She was sunk along with the German, *Kormoran*, whose crew were largely saved. The sunken cruiser was discovered in March, 2008.

On December 3rd , the Prime Minister said that the sloop, *HMAS Parramatta*, had been torpedoed and sunk while on escort duties, with a loss of 141 officers and men, out of a total complement of 161. She was re-supplying the garrison at Tobruk when attacked.

Mr Curtin said the loss of the two vessels was a heavy blow, but the nation and the Navy would be stiffened in determination and inspired to emulation by the example of self-sacrifice and devotion to duty.

OVER THE NEXT FEW DAYS ....

Cordell Hull insisted that Japan accept the demands for peaceful behaviour for the next three months. Japan said that it needed more time to think about them. There was no suggestion that the parallel play would ever stop.

Meanwhile, a huge Japanese fleet was positioning itself off the coast of Hawaii, and readying for battle, while the American fleet was sitting at anchor, stationary, and completely unsuspecting. It had no idea that **it** was the major target.

JAPANESE BOMBS FALL

On December 7th, the Japanese attacked the American fleet in Pearl Harbour at 8am with 183 aircraft. Much of the US Pacific fleet was destroyed, including the battleship *Arizona, Oklahoma*, and *West Virginia*. Only three battleships escaped, with minor damage. 170 aircraft were destroyed, while only nine Japanese planes were lost. A total of 2,403 American servicemen were killed. By chance, no American aircraft carriers had been in the Harbour at the time of the attack, a fact that depressed the Japanese Admiral Yamamoto.

At about the same time, and over the next week, Japanese planes, supported by land-forces, attacked at a dozen points throughout Asia and the Pacific, including the Philippines, Guam, Wake Island, Hong Kong, Thailand, Burma, Malaya, Singapore, Nauru, and the Ocean Islands. These attacks, over vast areas, were well co-ordinated and carried out in a masterful fashion, and instantly removed any conceptions that the Japanese were a "made-in-Japan" military power. Their subsequent invasions of all of these places, except Hawaii, were thoroughly successful, and over the next few days or weeks, all of them surrendered to Japanese rule.

The Allies were astonished at the audacity of the operations and surprised at the efficiency of execution. The politicians to a man reacted with huge quantities of vilification, and resolve. The Japanese had formally declared war on the US at the time of the Pearl Harbour attack, and the US retaliated a day later. Australia and Britain, and most of the Empire, did likewise. Hitler and Mussolini were thoroughly delighted to have a new chum in their fight against the Allies, and declared war against the US a few days later.

It was this latter declaration that brought the US into the European war. Had Hitler not declared war, it seems unlikely that the US would have entered the European fight. Germany might never have had to openly fight the Americans, and the course of world history would have been materially changed.

CHURCHILL'S NAVAL RE-INFORCEMENTS

Last month, Churchill had said that he was sending a number of heavy ships to Singapore. This force included the battleship, the *Prince of Wales*, and the pocket cruiser, *Repulse*. An aircraft carrier that was due to accompany them was in need of repairs, and so did not make the journey. These two vessels put to sea on December 8th, searching for a Japanese fleet that was reported to be off the Malayan coast. As they returned on December 10th, they were attacked by waves of torpedo-bombers. They had no air cover and so, being virtually defenceless, were both sunk with the loss of 800 sailors. A further 2,000 men were picked up by escorts.

This devastating loss brought home to everyone the fact that air power was crucial in this ocean-based war. Had the aircraft carrier been there, things would have been different. Had the 550 aircraft sent to Russia been there, again the results would have been different. As it was, however, this left Japan with an Imperial Navy of nine battleships and ten carriers in the Pacific, compared to the **current** US fleet of three American carriers and a small number of battleships.

OZ REACTION: WHO TO BLAME?

Churchill and Britain had been criticised by many for some faulty decisions, and indeed I have obliquely not been very supportive of him. Even now, we have the *SMH* doing a gentle carve-up, while counselling moderation.

"There is too much disposition in certain quarters to let despondency supervene upon the bewilderment and disquietude aroused by Japan's opening successes. Even worse is the tendency, in Australia and Britain, to exchange accusations regarding relative degrees of responsibility for unpreparedness to meet the Japanese onset in Malaya. Only the enemy can profit by such reproaches, at least so far as they concern the irrecoverable past. It is the dangerous present with which we have to deal, and emphasis on miscalculations and plain bungling must be unhelpful unless it contributes to the remedying of weaknesses in our existing position. That both political and strategical errors have been made is distressingly clear, and for these mistakes we have paid severely, especially in the loss of vital aerodromes, and, above all, of Penang. In consequence of these reverses, and the sinking of the two capital ships in the far Eastern Fleet, the threat to Singapore has become a grave reality. How to meet it is the problem which now presses grimly upon us.

"Singapore and Malaya lacked, and still lack, a sufficiency of war planes to cope with the Japanese air force. From this primary deficiency in their armament many of the troubles of the past fortnight have sprung. The obvious inference is that adequate air strength ought to have been provided in advance. As to this Sir Robert Brooke-Popham, in deploring "defeatist talk," said in Singapore on Monday that valuable supplies which might have gone to Malaya actually went to Libya and Russia, where they were desperately needed. Whether or not this is the whole, at least we may be sure that Britain will not lose an unnecessary moment in rushing re-enforcements of all kinds to the peninsula, and that America, despite her preoccupation with the Philippines, will not be unaware of the crucial importance of Singapore to the whole Allied position in the Pacific."

The Poms, however, had plenty of vocal defenders.

Letters, Clarity. I am and always have been an advocate of freedom of speech, liberty of the Press, and so on, and am a great believer in honest and constructive criticism, but surely the articles that have been appearing recently in a section of the Sydney Press do not come under this category. I am alluding particularly to articles concerning the Empire's strategy in the Far East, in which all the blame for any setbacks and losses we have sustained is attributed to faulty planning, stupidity, and muddle on the part of the authorities in England. The writers of these articles seem to think that the principal duty of those authorities is to safeguard Australia, quite forgetting, apparently, that for some time past the Empire's operations have been farflung, and that attention has to be given to all the different fronts or possible fronts such as Libya, Syria, Iran, Iraq,

Egypt, Turkey, France, Russia, Germany, Italy, China, and now the North Pacific.

When one comes to consider that only a little over two years ago the Empire was practically unarmed with the exception of a small army and a most efficient navy, and when one remembers the terrible losses we suffered on the Continent both in men and equipment, culminating in Dunkirk and the Battle for Britain, is it not really a most remarkable thing that we should now be in a position to carry on as we are doing all over the world, and should not this be placed to the credit of those in charge at home?

Surely what has been done notwithstanding most serious handicaps reflects great credit on those men, who certainly cannot be "stupid muddlers with one-track minds and pinheaded statesmen."

Letters, R M D. I am wondering if it is a kind of panic which, since Japan's entry into the war, has caused so many people, even a section of the Press, to "go" for England. Is it possible that we are so self-centred as to imagine that England's sole pre-occupation is our defence? Cannot we recognise and acknowledge her colossal task? With very little assistance she has fought in all the waters of the world; has driven back the invader from her shores; has undertaken difficult military tasks, ill-equipped because of the almost total loss in France and Belgium of her arms.

Now, by the industry of her people, she sends telling aid in tanks and arms and clothing, and one million pounds sterling for the Red Cross, to Russia.

England entered this war honourably, and for a principle. She did not wait to be attacked. Since she came in, lame and sick though she was after years of striving for peace, she has answered every call, given full and grateful thanks for every mite of help. The burden has been so great that only her broad shoulders, upheld and strengthened by the centuries, could have borne it; only her eyes have kept the dream.

OZ REACTION: THE GOVERNMENT

In the last three weeks of December, the Federal Government acted with great speed, and introduced a range of measures, sometimes wisely, and sometimes not.

Blackouts on sea ports. It declared that, for entities living in sea ports around the nation, it was illegal to allow lights at night to be seen from any distance out at sea. This order was effective immediately, and applied whether there was an air raid in progress on not.

Evacuation of school children. It announced that they would immediately investigate whether city children should be evacuated en masse to the country areas as had been done in Britain.

Air raid shelters. It, in conjunction with the States said they would provide funds for the construction of air-raid shelters and slit trenches in public parks and other areas of mass usage, such as playing fields. They issued how-to-do-it instructions for home owners who wanted to build their own shelters, and mandated that all large buildings must have shelters constructed.

Sport curtailed. Mid-week sport was declared illegal. This was particularly directed against the horse-racing industry.

Petrol usage. It, in conjunction with the States, urged people not to use their meagre petrol ration, but to keep it in their cars, ready to use for the common good in the event of an emergency.

Daylight saving was introduced nation-wide from January.

Taxes were increased by about 15 per cent.

No more tyres. Production of motor-car tyres for private use was prohibited. Similarly for bikes, and for floor coverings and matting. Production of golf balls and tennis balls was cut to 50 per cent.

Holidays restricted. All businesses and factories were to open for business during the upcoming Christmas period, except for the three festive days. For purposes of equity, this applied to all, whether they had work for employees or not.

No annual leave. Dr Evatt advised that he proposed to prevent workers from taking their annual leave for the duration of the War. Fortunately, the good sense of John Curtin prevailed, and he had to withdraw this policy proposal.

OZ REACTION: THE GENERAL PUBLIC

There were plenty of other changes implemented or proposed. As you might expect, many people objected to lots of these, and saw **other things** that might better be done. A sample of their Letters is included below. Again, **some** of these are sensible. See if you can pick the good ones.

Letters, William Jowitt. For black-outs, I find the simplest and most permanent method is to paint the outside of windows with a carriage-black paint, mixed with size. This is quite inexpensive – anyone can do the painting – and the job is permanent. If paper is used, it will require constant attention – it will peel off, get torn, and generally prove a nuisance.

Letters, V L Hardy. As Christmas mail imposes a severe strain on the postal authorities, with the necessity of additional staff working long hours, the public should be officially instructed to refrain, this year, from sending out the usual messages of greeting.

Letters, Seafarer. At 1pm on Sunday, seven days after the outbreak of war with Japan, there were no fewer than 67 private cars parked at Bronte Beach while their owners enjoyed the park and surf. As this beach is well served by trams from the city there is no justification for this waste of the most important item in Australia's war industry – namely, petrol.

Such waste must have the following effects: **One,** It will cost valuable lives and shipping replacing the petrol used. **Two,** it will make those who are genuinely doing their best in this war very disgruntled. **Three**, it will make that great body of "careless thinkers" decide that there cannot be much to worry about, after all. It must be emphasised again and again that shortage of fuel can bring Australia to a halt as far as this war is concerned, and quickly.

Letters, B, Glenbrook. Could not volunteers be called up to deal with child-birth accidents, which are common enough in normal life and tend to increase during shocks of war? Women of 50 and thereabouts who have reared families might be instructed by their doctors to act as emergency midwives where there are no certified midwives and no doctors in country villages and areas to which expectant mothers might be evacuated or where they might find themselves unexpectedly. In spite of our civilised state surprisingly few women know how to deal with a situation which primitive woman dealt with alone.

Letters, Alison Mackay. To save confusion during an air raid to those responsible for the care of wounded victims, the general public would be well advised to each wear an identification disc, similar to the ones issued to the fighting forces. These discs could be made quickly and at little cost.

Letters, Jessie Donovan. As a mother with two small children living in a vulnerable area, I am naturally interested in evacuation schemes. So far, all we know is that families are to be evacuated to country towns. This does not take into account working mothers (many of them in essential war work), who couldn't possibly leave their work to take children to the country. We want to know if whole schools, kindergartens, day nurseries, etc., are to be evacuated as units? There is no reason why big homes, guest houses, etc, cannot be taken over for the duration, and kindergartens evacuated with their staffs.

This evacuation problem is worrying thousands of mothers. We want our children safe now. The sooner our children are safe, the sooner will women pull their very considerable weight behind the war effort. Women must and will play a big role in this war. They will take their men's places in the factories, in relieving men in the Army. They will do all that is asked of them, but in the interests of efficiency and morale, they must know that their children are safe from the bombing planes.

Letters, Widow with Schoolboy Son. I am disgusted by people paying exorbitant rentals for lease of a single room in the country to save their skins from our enemies. Perhaps, if they paused to think they would utilise those hundreds of pounds in helping to keep the enemy out of the country instead of running away. Individuality should not count now with any true citizen.

Letters, Audrey Coutts. The Widow should realise that everyone is different, and their circumstances are different. I too am a widow, living right in Sydney, and right next to what would be a target for enemy bombing. If incendiary bombs fell on the target, we would have no chance.

So I want to move elsewhere. The only place I can afford go, is the country. Is this so bad?

There are a thousand reasons to move under these circumstances. I hope the good lady will rethink her pointless judgements.

Letters, Dorothy Knox, Principal, Presbyterian Ladies' College, Pymble. It is possible that, in the event of an actual emergency arising, a small portion of the college property, as well as many other properties, may be required for national purposes. If and when that should be so, the normal activities of the college will still continue.

Parents will be notified immediately of any modification of existing plans.

Members of the general public are asked to refrain from circulating false and misleading statements issued on the authority of a friend of a friend of "someone who knows". It is right and proper that our Government should carry out its task of planning and providing for an emergency. It is greatly to be deprecated that idle gossips should cause confusion and inconvenience, thus making more difficult the task of those already carrying a grave responsibility.

At present, we have pleasure in informing the public that the college is not a maternity hospital, nor military barracks, nor an aerodrome.

Letters, R Yates. I add my protest against the dropping of the Gilbert and Sullivan opera *Mikado* from the Sydney season. The fact that it is centred around **Japanese** society is not at all pertinent.

It is if fact engaging and first class entertainment. It has stood the test of time, and can be guaranteed to attract a big audience.

A few, just a few, fanatics want it banned. We should not let the tail shake the dog.

SUMMING UP 1941

Australia at the start of 1941 had no idea that it was vulnerable to attack. Our eyes were turned to Europe, and the bombing of London, and the battles in Libya. Then on to the terrible events in Greece and Crete. After that, the German invasion of Russia, and now the Russian fightback. But the idea that Australia might be involved in a war in the Pacific that came to our own shores just was not considered. In fact, only a month ago, all the leaders in the nation were still fixed on European events, and more or less ridiculed any thoughts of Japanese aggression causing us any worry. And in any case, the impregnable Singapore, and the might of the British Navy, would keep us safe.

Now, the penny was starting to drop. The above suggestions were a sample from hundreds of Letters that swamped every newspaper, and their diversity tells us that people from all walks of life were stirred up. And they wanted do **something**. No one was certain what was really needed, but if a leader came forward and gave them the right direction, the people of Australia were in the mood to at last pitch in and give of their utmost.

John Curtin next year, in 1942, proved to be such a leader. This level-headed, unpretentious politician gained the trust of the people of Australia, and led them through the many and frightening days of **worry and despair**, and **hope and courage**, that bedevilled Australia in the most perilous year in its history.

In 1944, the Japs in the Pacific and the Nazis in Europe were just about beaten. Sydney was invaded by rats, and there were lots of Yankee soldiers in all our cities. Young girls were being corrupted by the Yanks and by war-time freedom, and clergy were generous with their advice to them. Germany was invaded, but that did not stop the Doodlebugs dropping on London.

In 1946, the War was over, but not rationing.

Some products were rationed until 1950. The Brits were starving, war brides were pouring out of Britain as fast as we could bring them. TB was on the increase, and a long-term polio epidemic was just starting. Our nurses were underpaid and overworked, War-crimes trials were catching up with villains in Europe and here. As a result, we found out about Sandakan where only six men out of 1,650 Aussie POW's survived Japanese brutality. Pit whistles reduced some of us to tears.

****

Books for Mum and Dad and Aunt and Uncle and cousins and family and friends and work and everyone else.

Don't forget a good read and chuckle for yourself.

In 1948, there was no shortage of rationing and regulation, as the Labor government tried to convince voters that war-time restrictions should stay. Immigration Minister Calwell was staunchly supporting our White Australia Policy, though he would generously allow five coloured immigrants from each Asian nation to settle here every year. Burials on Saturday were banned. Rowers in Oxford were given whale steak to beat meat rationing.

In 1960, Oz women were said to be drunks, professional tennis came via Jack Kramer to this fair land. The concept of male nurses was raised, Arthur Calwell's dead hand fell on the Labour Party, William Dobell was said to have tricked the Art World on April Fools Day, and two especially gory murders were committed in Maitland. And, can you believe it, a few men were admitted to hospitals during the labours of women. Has the new idea of the equality of the sexes gone too far?

****

There are 33 Titles in this Series

They cover the 33 years from 1939 to 1971

Details are available from www.boombooks.biz

Printed in Australia
AUHW021512271021
354375AU00058B/445

9 780648 771647